To my wife, who has been my mutual partner in living
into the content of this book.

To the Leading Community of Axiom Church for sharing
in the work of these rooted practices.

SUBTERRANEAN

SUBTERRANEAN

Why the Future of the Church Is Rootedness

Dan White Jr.

Foreword by JR Woodward
Afterword by David E. Fitch

CASCADE *Books* · Eugene, Oregon

SUBTERRANEAN
Why the Future of the Church Is Rootedness

Cascade Books
An Imprint of Wipf and Stock Publishers
199 W. 8th Ave., Suite 3
Eugene, OR 97401

www.wipfandstock.com

ISBN 13: 978-1-4982-1953-2

Cataloguing-in-Publication Data

White, Dan, Jr.

    Subterranean : why the future of the church is rootedness / Dan White Jr.

    xxii + 174 p. ; 23 cm. Includes bibliographical references.

    ISBN 13: 978-1-4982-1953-2

    1. Mission of the church. 2. Christianity and culture. I. Title.

BV601.8 W44 2015

Manufactured in the U.S.A.   07/31/2015

Contents

Illustrations

Foreword

FROM THE MOMENT WE could speak, we have been asking questions; it's the way we grow in understanding. When we asked our parents a question we were not often satisfied with the first answer they gave. So we followed up with the classical question, why? After hearing our parents respond, we quickly weighed their response with our current knowledge, and within less than a second, we probably asked another question, "Why is that?" If you've interacted with kids, you undoubtedly have lived this experience. We have engaged in the art of asking questions from the moment we could speak. At some point in our youth, however, we begin to pick up the notion that "right" answers might be more important than good questions. Our culture conditions us through reward and punishment that having the right answers is preferred.

Much of our education trains us to give quick answers. We pass our classes in school with better grades if we've produced the right answers. We pass our driving test because of right answers. Very few of us are nurtured to ask good questions and keep asking good questions. We have learned that answers gain respect, while questions might display ignorance. Oh yes, occasionally we were told, "No question is too dumb." But quietly we were thinking, "Only the ignorant ask questions." The consistent conditioning we experienced in every other part of our lives was that the smart have instant answers, and the not-so-smart are left with questions. Yet, the art of learning to ask good questions is one of the more meaningful skills we can develop as humans. Asking questions assumes curiosity and a hunger to learn. Engaging in the practice of thoughtful questions will place us in a humble posture that is rewarded with deeper understanding and greater wisdom. The doorway to discovery is entered through asking thoughtful questions.

People who master the art of asking questions become skilled at revealing the heart of the matter—what is really going on under the surface. They ask questions that provoke us to consider how our underlying assumptions about life and ministry may lend themselves to "unintended consequences."

Jesus' ministry was marked by asking good questions. Growing up in Jewish culture, he was schooled in the art of asking questions. When, at twelve years old, Jesus was traveling with his family back from Jerusalem to celebrate Passover, Mary and Joseph thought Jesus was with them, but they traveled a whole day before they realized he was missing. Three days later, what do they find Jesus up to? He was "sitting among the teachers, eagerly listening to them and *asking them questions.*"

Jesus matured in the art of question-asking and he practiced it often. In fact, asking questions was one of the fundamental ways he shaped his disciples for the work of the kingdom. When he interacted with the crowds, he would typically ask a question following a parable. When the Pharisees or Sadducees posed questions to Jesus in attempt to trick him and make him look bad in public, seldom did Jesus respond with a direct answer. More often he would ask them a question.

Why did he do this? Jesus understood that questions help guide people to the beauty of the truth. He knew that good questions expose false assumptions. He knew that before we can reconstruct a proper view of reality, our false underlying assumptions (often uncritically adapted) must first be deconstructed. Good questions lead us to the truth, and ultimate truth is found in God incarnate in the person of Jesus.

As you read this book, you will discover that Dan White Jr. is adept in the art of asking careful but potent questions. Throughout this book, he asks questions that will provoke us to look at the underlying assumptions we have about ourselves, our ministry ambitions, and about how to be the church in the world. As a prophetic pastor, Dan is willing to ask difficult questions of himself first, and then pose them to the world around him, potentially turning it upside down. Dan is interested in more than tipping over the apple cart with questions; he is interested in helping the church find the way of Jesus.

The questions weaving through *Subterranean* are pointing us to the concrete person of Christ, not an abstract idea. When we see Jesus, we see God "taking on flesh and bones and moving into the neighborhood." Dan employs the tool of *good questions* to help us recover this Jesus-like posture that our churches have potentially given lip service to. If you are satisfied with the status quo, then don't read this book. Dan, like a reliable guide, will question your underlying assumptions and invite you into real reform.

In Part I of this book, Dan deconstructs the more popular versions of the church today. The questions he asks are the questions he soaked in himself when he lived under some of his old assumptions. Don't move too quickly through this part. There are social forces at work in our leadership and ministries that need to be questioned. Before solid reconstruction can take place, deconstruction must do its work. Be assured, as you continue on to read Part II, you will find Dan gradually engaging in the work of reconstruction and renewal. So press on.

As you journey through Part II, you will realize that Dan has opened space with his questions to enable us to follow the Incarnate One, who left a realm in which time and space had no consequence. Jesus did this in order to live in a particular time, with a particular people, in a particular place. This is the pattern for what the more *rooted* church looks like, and Dan offers offer you and your church tools and pathways for being this kind of Christian community. Dan has been practicing ministry with these new foundational convictions for some time now, so he has tested wisdom from on-the-ground application.

The church is in a desperate state and this book will not pummel you with cool ideas; instead, it will unfold the essential character for what the kingdom of God looks like sprouting up in a local place. The kingdom of God is like a mustard seed. Jesus illustrated what the prophet Zechariah said, "Don't despise the day of small beginnings," for in time this tiniest of seeds, when nourished, develops roots and grows into a tree. This pattern has deeply influenced Dan's ongoing ministry and it has the potential to renovate the presence of the people of God in the world. Honestly, this book is basic in its premise, "What does it mean to be the rooted church?"—yet the work to recover rootedness is not a simple task. That is why this book is so important for the future of the church, as we need to move beyond simplistic, fast-growth, big-impact, and latest-trend answers to truly recover those vital roots.

As you read, be sure to underline the questions that speak to you. Then ask yourself, why does this question stand out to me? What is God saying to me through this?

Record those questions, ponder those questions, dialogue with others about those questions, and I assure you, you will grow in real knowledge.

But if you want to grow in wisdom, you have to ask yourself a couple more questions: In light of what God's Spirit is saying to me, what does God want me to practice? How should I put this into practice with others?

Jesus said, "The kingdom of God is for those who are like children." Like its title, this book will dive deep. Be willing "like a child" to learn afresh what it means to join the subterranean movement of the in-breaking kingdom of God.

JR Woodward
National Director, V3 Church Planting Movement

Preface

IT'S PROBABLY NOT A great marketing move to admit you are not a natural writer. Being a writer was never on my bucket list. Since I was nineteen years of age and scanning over the last twenty years, all that I've ever wanted to be was a pastor. I've always preferred the exhaustive work of being with people more than the exhaustive work of putting pen to paper. I'm an introvert, so dwelling with people with hopes of transforming together has seemed to require all of the energy I could muster. To write just sounded like an extra burden. Yet over the years I have consistently journaled. Reading my journal exposes my thoughts, my tossing and turning with ministry. My journal entries show a pattern over the last fifteen years; the pattern of an annoying inner dialogue that was growing in strength and would not be alleviated by journaling. Some of my inner dialogue reflected the wandering chats my wife and I would have late into the night about the nature of the church and its future. As a called and career pastor with the wonderful privilege of ministering in various denominations, conservative or progressive, liturgical or contemporary, Bible-preaching or justice loving, large budgets or lean budgets, all my reflections were piecing together around some core common issues. My meager inner dialogue came screaming to the forefront when I had the opportunity of a lifetime to lead a successful megachurch. As a relatively young pastor this is what you fantasize about, right? Every vocational field has a ladder to climb, whether named or not named. A busting-at-the-seams church with all of the trimmings was supposed to be the prize for all my theological studying, conference attending, and leadership-skill building. So I glared the opportunity in the face, ready to walk into the promised land, and realized something wasn't right.

God had been taking a jackhammer ever so gently to the foundation of my ecclesiology, which was rattling the bones of my self-understanding as a ministry leader. It was evident in my journal entries and in my percolating conversations with some close companions. My conscience was increasingly uncomfortable with what it meant to be a "successful" pastor and I was uncomfortable with the cultural description of what it meant to be a successful church. Success, though never stated overtly, was dependent on many of the factors that made me the high school quarterback or earned me public speaking awards or helped me pull off huge fund-raising events. I had personality, charm, and could infuse energy into a room. As a decent communicator I knew how to draw a crowd. Honestly, my framework for being the church was biased by my shiny skill set.

Rewind, as a couple of previous summers I experienced a disruption. I decided to read through the early church letters afresh, asking one simple question: *What is the church?* I wasn't looking for sermon material; I just wanted to see the forest for the trees. With my Bible and a five-by-seven notebook alongside I meandered through Acts, Corinthians, Ephesians, and Thessalonians with that question written at the top of every page. After a few weeks, I remember vividly sitting in a lawn chair, head resting in the palm of my hands, realizing I was reading something unfamiliar to me and it was unraveling me. I've studied all this before, slicing, dicing, and cooking it up to deliver to others, yet on an experiential level it looked strange and foreign. I had not known experientially the ecclesiastical life found in the New Testament, now scribbled in my notebook. I had a genuine sense of feeling like a sham, like a carpenter who somehow avoided ever being in the woodshop. I had versed myself in organizational principles, better church methods, communication tactics, and research on relevancy, and it had drifted me away from the axioms of being the body of Christ. I don't mean body of Christ as a Sunday event and a midweek program, I mean body of Christ as unfolded in the imperfect community of *oikos*. *Oikos* is the Greek word for household. However, its meaning is much broader than what we typical give to the definition of household. For us it means those who live under one roof. However, for those living in the Ancient Near East during the time of Christ it came to mean the *metaphoric* family that intentionally oriented around each other, in a particular place. The *oikos* is the imperfect, messy, relational, organic but organized amoeba of the first-century church. *Oikos* was the hot mess of God's in-breaking kingdom that supported early Christians for mission in a city, for maturing in love, for the practice of the Eucharist, for the collision of racial diversity, for resistance to paganism, and for being shaped as disciples. This is where the activity was. There was no other option. This was church undiluted and I knew very little of this alternative life exposed and explained by the Apostle Paul. I had lead many discipleship programs, participated in many small group Bible studies and preached many captivating sermons, but very little of it inched me closer to the grit and grime of *oikos*. I'm not an idealist believing we can duplicate what occurred 2,000 years ago, but I certainly believe something primordial needs to be resurrected in our efficiency-constricted, personality-driven, entertainment-addicted, community-starved, size-obsessed culture. Sitting there that sunny afternoon I was being reinvigorated but in some ways paralyzed. I felt the hammer of change pounding away at my identity but I did not know how to move into the spaciousness of practice. So for the next few years I privately churned in conversation with my gifted wife. I did my best to serve faithfully at the ministry posts God had given me. Everything came to head for me when I was offered that "successful" pastoral position at a megachurch.

All my dreaming and ruminating about a new but old way forward as church was going to be tested, was going to be pressed through a gauntlet. For me the acceptance of that successful church job was a temptation offering me a shortcut around what God had been teaching me. Yet I was not emotionally ready for the cost. I wanted that job so desperately but was so conflicted that I decided to get away for three days to pray, fast, and get some clarity. I got a cheap hotel room in an adjacent city and began seeking wisdom. By the end of day two I came up completely dry; my prayers were cluttered and my headspace was no clearer. I found nothing at the bottom of the barrel of my mind. So out of pure frustration I decided to go for a walk downtown that night. It was the dead of winter. I bundled up like an Eskimo and began stumbling around the city with no direction and a grumbling attitude. On my walk I came across a homeless brother sitting up against a building on the icy sidewalk. As I approached him, he waved me over. I hesitantly came closer and he motioned to the ground saying "sit down." I sat down and I could see his breath puffing under the dim street light, as he turned and asked, "What are you afraid of?" I responded with a caught-off-guard "Huh?" My new homeless friend responded with quoting "I will never leave you nor forsake you. Be strong and courageous. . . . Be careful to obey the law I've given you; do not turn from it to the right or to the left, then you will be prosperous and successful. Have I not commanded you? Be strong and courageous. Do not be afraid; do not be discouraged, for God will be with you wherever you go" (Josh 1:5–7). I was aghast. Horror gushed into my heart and I knew what was happening. I was a Baptist boy but this holy interruption was hard to pass off as merely a crazy home-less guy. He was a vessel of truth. The message was clear. I was riddled with fear and my insides began to split open. I cried tears of honesty for the first time in a long time. My homeless friend got up slowly, using my shoulder as a crutch, and moseyed down the street around the corner. I sat there and I could feel my cowardice. I feared failing, I feared not making any money, I feared not being successful. My ego was in an Olympic wrestling match with the idea of success. God spoke through a homeless brother to break up the hard ground of my soul to make space for absorbing the fresh water of new directions. Soon I drove home, walked in the door, and immediately told my wife what had happened. She said, "We can't be afraid." So I turned down the job the following day. Fast forward, and it hasn't been easy, but I've been attempting to practice a more rooted way of being the people of God in the world. I have had the joy of making this trek with others. My own blue-collar practice is dripping from the pages of this book and it is by no means perfect. I've tried to be honest throughout about my own inner temper tantrums to reorient around rootedness.

I recall that story because it is my story and it has framed much of the issues I will press into. I believe the future of the church is a rooted one; one that submerges itself in community, in neighborhoods, and in focused faithfulness. The recovery of a rooted church will collide with real leaders, trained in real "success" strategies that have formed real personal images of being significant. Everything about rootedness will collide with our inner dependency on versions of success built on personality, expediency, and efficiency. When pressing into the future of the church our own leader-ship habits must go through a maximum dynamic pressure. Maximum dy-namic pressure is what a space shuttle goes through at the point it punches through the atmosphere. The integrity of the shuttle is taxed, exposing the craftsmanship and character of its construction.

Is the church of the future dependent on magnetic personalities or rooted practice?

THE COLLAPSE

The Western societal structure was shocked in the decade following the turn of the millennium, by the bombings of the World Trade Center, the collapse of the economy, and the growing difficulty of attaining the

American dream. Rather than a carnival of prosperity we find ourselves discouraged in our dashed hopes, secluded from each other, and strangely detached from contentment, even though we have more at our fingertips than ever. We are sputtering to apprehend a sense of self, an established identity. So we reach into the panoply of accessories to be labeled as a video gamer, a granola mom, a starving musician, an environmental activist, a Jesus freak, a popular blogger, a gym rat, etc. These descriptors offer some bobbing life preservers in the turbulent social ocean, but we know it, we feel it . . . they don't offer us rootedness. The church in the last decade has tapped its best leaders for solutions and they've responded with louder preaching, worship bathed in light shows, candles and incense, and a behemoth array of Christian living programs. We practice a neurotic ecclesiology, anxious around our personality, whether that's to be a strong preaching church, a strong worship church, a strong family church, a strong justice church, or even a strong biker church. Will people gravitate towards our personality? We read research telling us what Millennials want and then attempt to engineer experiences that will appeal to them. This causes us to bounce about like chameleons. Or, to shift metaphors, we are like an insecure adolescent wondering if people will like the new shirt we just bought.

All of this running around after fads is bankrupting our rootedness. We have not scrutinized the Trojan horse of our church ingenuity for what violence it does in our midst. This was the algorithm between all my church experiences; the church has become *uprooted*. When we are uprooted we are more dependent on personalities for energy, more fragmented from each other, more opportunity-chasing and less faithful to the beauty and brokenness in our neighborhoods.

A GROUNDSWELL

There is a growing groundswell of people around the country looking for a new way to be human, with other people, in a particular place. The Christendom complex is crumbling and rather than bailing on the church, some are reconstituting their commitment to the first seedlings of what made the church peculiar and powerful. This is not a project that worships nostalgia. Instead, it is a sobered reach back into history for guidance and forward application. There is a primal recognition that we are to be placed firmly with each other, with a long-term mission, with a passion for where we live. This burgeoning movement is not made in the kiln of the consumerism

factory that cooks up new techniques for being a trendier church. Rootedness resists that arms race of "cool." Rootedness seeks to plunge below
the buffet of choices, magnetic personalities, and manufactured buzz into
a subterranean way to be the church carrying with it an unwavering incarnational creed.

THE UPROOTED CHURCH

The book is divided into two halves that reflect the route my own formation
took. First, we'll walk through a sticky patch of "sacred scrutiny" on how
we are *uprooted*. We'll do some essential deconstruction, leveling the land
for our future work in the second half. We'll expose the forces that have
needled their elbow in the spine of the church, causing us to bend towards:

Excessive Personality

The competition is on to be a significant church. Whoever is bigger and
bolder often wins in the court of who's more observably impressive. Our
ambitions to be significant have pushed us to become disinterested in and
potentially have disdain for embracing limits. In our surge to build significant churches we've unintentionally *severed* the character of *presence*.

Extracted Perception

Information is king in our social economy. To know more is to be more and
is to be equipped for competing in the world. So creating efficient faucets
that gush out spiritual information has become a priority. In our surge to
download information to hungry learners we've unintentionally *severed* the
character of *practice*.

Expedited Production

Our modern imagination for having an impact channels most of our energy on how quickly something can take off. Restraint in our ambitious
goals seems silly and only slows us down. There is a demand within us for
production and production immediately. In our surge for microwave-speed
impact we've unintentionally *severed* the character of *patience*.

I hope to tell a convincing tale of how we've coalesced with these social forces and how they are deteriorating our incarnational nervous system as a church.

THE ROOTED CHURCH

The second half of this book will be more hopeful, offering some essential helps for being a subterranean church. We will move toward a reconstruction of a radical rootedness. We'll plunge into three overlapping practices:

Rooted Fidelity

Faithfulness is the primary muscle formed and shaped in the first-century Christians for the work of cultivating the kingdom of God. The muscle of fidelity has become neglected, no longer undergoing a daily exercise routine. We've become increasingly more faithful to our own individualized spiritual experiences that demand very little from us. Fidelity is the concept of unfailing loyalty to something exterior to our own wants and putting that loyalty into consistent practice for sake of subverting the social forces that seek to erode us.

Rooted Locality

We are made to find our identities in a particular place. The incarnation of God in Christ has boated ahead of us and created a wake for us to follow in regards to living locally. There is a labyrinth of life and culture in our neighborhoods that must be recognized, respected, and reoriented around. The future of the church must strip away all of the gimmicks in order to dwell in a place with the flesh-and-blood people living there.

Rooted Community

We are made to belong to people and become new with people. From the beginnings of the creation story we are made for interdependence with others. New creation is the work of cultivating community; it is an all-out rebellion against the cultural surge of self-reliance, isolation, and self-actualization.

In no way is this book exhaustive in drawing us into rootedness. I've attempted to simplify large concepts, theological narratives, and my own application into something accessible. We are uprooted and the questions we must explore are not mere landscaping. We cannot landscape while there is an earthquake on a plate-tectonic level. Let's submerge past the appearance of our best methods and creative techniques to recover what will nourish the church; we need to go *subterranean*.

Acknowledgments

THIS BOOK IS SITUATED within my own story; the formative events, questions, and explorations of it. My own experience obviously colors my hypothesis in the book. I'm at peace with this reality. I've never been one comfortable in the halls of academia. Seeing myself as a blue-collar practitioner first and foremost certainly shapes the content of this book. I have an allergic reaction to literature prescribing solutions that were boiled in mere ruminating or manufactured within an ivory tower. Ideas are candy in our consumer society. Ideation has become a best-selling meme, but earthed-out practice *with* others is like the rarity of spotting a Sumatran tiger in the wild. I concede that others have better ideas that hypothetically could progress us beyond our current circumstances. Maybe I'm different, but my best ideas always get harangued and humbled when pressed out into practice with others. This is what I've attempted to discipline myself to in *Subterranean*. I did not want to write anything that has not had to run through the obstacle course of practice. This limits the scope of the book and maybe the appeal. What the church could be stirs me up, but it's the daily rhythm of being the church with real people in a real place with a real mission that has rewired my DNA.

There are many authors who have influenced me deeply over the years. These include John Howard Yoder, Alan Hirsch, John Perkins, Christine Pohl, Dallas Willard, Dietrich Bonhoeffer, Scot McKnight, and Jean Vanier. But my most formative spiritual directors have been mentors and disciplers in real time. Those directors formed me in various ways as I observed parts of their lives and gave them permission to apprentice me. I owe much to Dr. George Snyder (rabbi), who shared numerous cups of coffee with me dialoguing about historical Judaism and the concerns of a young pastor. The late Jim Dejidas impacted my formation greatly as he affirmed me and equipped me to press into urban ministry challenges. John Hawco was a significant up-close spiritual force in my life-modeling love for God and fiery passion for the ecclesia. Marlene June Eissens spent many hours with me discussing and discerning emotionally healthy ways for me to be in ministry. Not all of my disciplers would agree fully with the premise of this book, but I want to acknowledge the gift of their influence on my development.

I want to thank my parents, Dan and Elly, for being emotional and practical support in my venture to plant a church. Growing up in a love-filled home gave me a sense of being that still gives me stability today.

Finally, my wife and friend Tonya has for twenty years loved me faithfully as well as graciously addressed regions of my life that needed maturing. Without the strength of her emotional and intellectual touch I would be unstable. Thanks also to my son, Daniel, who had patience with me, always asking "When will you be done working on *Subterranean*?" My own family has provided me belonging in the harshness of the world while simultaneously compelling me to practice more rooted ways of being the church.

PART ONE

The Suspended State of the Church

1

Hotels or Trees

GROWING UP, MY FAMILY had a huge willow tree in the backyard. The tree defined the entirety of that grassy space as its sleepy branches drooped down, creating a canopy to play under. I scaled that tree many times, finding a better vantage point for squirt gun wars waged with neighborhood kids. The neck of that tree was as thick as a car, so it created a perfect disappearing spot when playing hide-and-go-seek with my brother. When I flashback that tree was almost like a character in my life. Its whimsical creature-like presence was a sprawling fixture in the adventures of my childhood. Just about a year ago I drove through that neighborhood after being away for thirty-plus years. The neighborhood looked quite different, as the houses had been remodeled and a new development of stores was now eating up a portion of the block. Yet towering in the same space was that massive willow tree with the same big sleepy look, as if it had been waiting for me to come back and lean up against its trunk. I was quite surprised it hadn't been cut down. Maybe someone else had appreciated its presence.

WILLOW TREE

FANTASTICAL OR FAITHFUL

In my travels, I've seen some impressive human-made structures that obviously required much time and money to construct. The architectural precision of the Atomium Hotel in Brussels is fantastical: it's an almost sci-fi building, made up of seven suspended spheres, connected by twenty tubes to wander through, each offering a panoramic view of the city. The dream of the hotel at its building in 1958 was to inspire humanity toward a better future, characterized by harmony, brilliance, and progress.[1] The almost-otherworldly shape of the structure was an invitation to celebrate the dawn of tomorrow's world. Yet for all its elegant engineering I find the symbol of stacked shiny steel not prepared for the real longings of the future. It is the power of that willow tree in my childhood backyard that stands more as an unassuming symbol for what the future aches for. Our ingenuity, intelligent ideas, and cutting-edge approaches cannot replace the souls craving being rooted. We can build churches higher to the sky and host worship events that explode in stadium-size emotion, but the missional future of the church needs a deep reflection on and recovery of its roots. The tree is a delicate organism in our technocratic world. Human progress could cut down that tree tomorrow, but nothing can replace the existence that tree testifies to. That tree echoes a primordial story.

ATOMIUM HOTEL

1. "Futuristic & Universal," www.atomium.be/History.aspx.

The Kingdom Tree

Trees are a leading symbol in ancient religion and in modern times. Trees are living organisms that often outlast the brevity of humans and the animal population. Trees are at the pinnacle of the plant world, transforming the earth from a barren state into a place capable of supporting other forms of life. They tower when we fall and they are still alive when we die. Our planet has the magnificence of the mahogany trees in Honduras, the Douglas fir evergreen trees forming a canopy in the Pacific Northwest, the pines in the Black Hills in South Dakota, and the Ivenack Oak, located in Poland and now 800 years old. Trees are enchanting in their personality as they grow slow but grow strong. As we lean back and look up, they incite wonder. Our finger tips can feel their rough bark and our noses can smell their sweet scent. Their earthbound presence is also undeniable.

Trees are tremendous and magical bodies that have occupied a unique place in Jewish thought, closely relating to man's relationship with a life-support system. The Jewish Midrash stresses this importance for ancient Israel to prepare new lands for the long term: "When God created the world, His first action was to plant trees, as it is written, 'and God planted trees in Eden.' So [for] you, too, when you enter the land of Israel, planting trees should be your first involvement."[2] Trees are symbolic of a sustainable life that nurtures other life. Stroll through the Scriptures and you'll uncover an emblematic appearance of trees, with their qualities of perseverance, beauty, and care for those who linger under their branches. Over one hundred times trees are emphasized. God's faithful work in the world is frequently illustrated in the symbolism of a tree.

In Genesis it says, "out of the ground the Lord God grew trees . . . and placed in the midst of the garden the Tree of Life" (Gen 2:9). So in the opening sequences of the Bible a tree immediately indicates God's presence. The Tree of Life stands at the center. *The tree declares God is here.* Not only is God here but his presence is secured and soaring in the midst, sourcing life to the rest of the wild habitat.

The fig tree is also a species mentioned in (Gen 3:7) and later the fig tree enables someone to view Jesus when Zacchaeus climbs a sycamore (a type of fig tree). The tree not only symbolizes God's presence, but also helps us get a better view.

2. Wolff and Neril, "Trees, Torah, and Caring for the Earth."

Another distinct tree that makes an appearance is the olive tree. In the life of Israel the olive tree is symbolic of their role in God's plans. "Behind and underneath all of this is a holy, God-planted, God-tended tree. If the primary root of the tree is holy, there's bound to be some holy fruit" (Rom 11:15–25). Additionally, the oil from the olive tree acts as the fuel used in clay lamps, supplying the tabernacle with light (Exod 30:24–25).[3] The manifestation of a tree is a distinct representation of God's sustenance.

Isaiah declares prophetically about the new kingdom community that will be assembled by the Messiah, "The Spirit of God is on me, sending me to speak good news to the poor, healing for the heartbroken and freedom to all captives . . . they will be like 'Oaks of Righteousness' planted by God to display his goodness" (Isa 61:3) The tree offers us a new identity that testifies to the creator God.

Standing at the center of time is the cross, a tree where God shockingly dies, naked and vulnerable. God is murdered and allows his enemies to spill his blood down the lumber of a tree. It is here that we get our most unusual picture of how the tree symbolizes God's finer work in the world. The tree is an enigma in the way it explains God's collision with humanity. There is a supernatural botany to God's movement into the world, establishing shalom on earth as it is in heaven.

Finally, in the new city recorded in Revelation 21:9–27 we get a sweeping portrayal of the renewal of all things. In the intersection of streets, on the other side of the river, stands that original Tree of Life quietly and powerfully present, bearing fruit as it brings healing to all the peoples of the world.[4] This tree's roots go deep but its branches rise over the entire earth as its leaves scatter the will of God. Ultimately the tree is well suited to symbolize King Jesus' rule in the in-breaking kingdom.

THE KINGDOM OF GOD IS LIKE A TREE

This tree orients everything. The entire world, my city, my neighborhood, my community, and my life is in the shade of God's in-breaking kingdom. Like a tree, the kingdom brings life into lifeless situations, giving off oxygen to those needing to breathe in grace, grafting itself to a specific location, sprouting at a pace the eye cannot always observe, and persevering through the harshest of seasons. The tree is rooted to this earth. Jesus' entire life was

3. Wahm, "Significant Trees in the Bible."
4. Taylor-Weiss, "What Trees Mean in the Bible."

a kingdom commencement of heaven's rule coming to this soil and sod for the revealing of God in our places. Jesus-life is not an abstract principle; it is an earthbound collision with people, with places, and with systems saturated in a historical reality. From the very moment Jesus begins to gather ragamuffin disciples they are recruited towards this earthbound work. Jesus picks up the long, drama-filled story of the Israelite people chosen to be the tangible presence of Yahweh in the world and recalibrates it towards being a grounded church for all tribes. *Church* is a loaded word, flooding our minds with all kinds of images from the last thousand years. Yet Jesus and his disciple movement are the first seedlings for the relational infrastructure of a church. In Jesus, God is gathering people under his reign to participate in the renewal of the world. God's reign is concerned with undoing humankind's Tower-of-Babel posture that oppresses the weak and creates isolation. God's reign recovers our desires from the burning heap of self-indulgence and restores our identities as loved ones who love others. The kingdom is not an esoteric idea or a far-off place in the clouds or Christianized government or a 501c3 doing social good. The kingdom of God is the people of God submitting to the King's will in the place they are called to dwell. The kingdom tree sprouts up in the concentrated place where we seek to be the ecclesia, meaning, to be the gathered body of Jesus-followers committed to each other, committed to a place, and committed to the remembrance of Jesus as true King. The kingdom of God drives us deep into the church and the church drives us deep into the world. A kingdom community has no greater calling than to cultivate its active life together in light of this truth. We are invited to massage a richer and thicker reality of this into human imaginations. There is nothing truer than God in Christ's work to cultivate his kingdom tree in a place. Everything, every last inch of our living, is to reorient around this supernatural collision of heaven and earth; yet let's be honest, it takes disciplined vision to maintain focus on this sometimes hard-to-measure project. When you compare the attention grabbing, glitz and glam of the Atomium Hotel in Europe to the slow and sleepy growth of a tree, it takes a different set of eyes to see what is infinitely more valuable.

UNASSUMING PRESENCE

The Tree of Life will not compete and clamor for attention. It will grow in subversive, quiet, and even hidden ways. It does not leverage typical channels of human marketing and mass-culture hype in the form of powerful personalities, political offices, and perceptive strategies. The kingdom of God is different than humankind's version of success. The church's fascination with modern progresses, sexier methods, and new social innovations can create disinterest in something as meek as the movement of the kingdom of God. When we think "kingdom" we often conjure up images of mighty armies triumphing over their foes or a wealthy family creating a dynasty. The idea of kingdom can lean towards the acquisition of more power, more popularity, and more capital in the form of people. This cultural current is running through many church leaders and subsequently many churches, with a currency that has traumatized our love for the mustard-seed smallness of God's style of work. Much of our modeling of "kingdom" looks like the acclaimed hero, the awarded philanthropist, or the fastest-growing start-up company. But the kingdom of God is not a lesson in how to grab attention for the glory of God. Rather, it's a lesson in how to get smaller to move meaningfully into the mess of human brokenness.

Honestly, Jesus wouldn't make a great modern politician, a good visioneer, or successful stage personality. His most central message of the kingdom of God is often clouded and cloaked in the language of parables, fictional stories.[5] This drove his disciples crazy! In Matthew 13:34 the writer makes the point that "Jesus did not say anything without using parables." A parable would often end with the refrain "whoever has ears, let him hear." A parable would often include a hidden message that would be accessible to some and confusing to others.[6] At one point the disciples share their absolute frustration with this approach. "Why do you speak in parables like this?" As if to say "Jesus, why are you doing this? You're telling stories but nobody is getting your point, can you find a clearer, cleaner, more captivating way to communicate?" I find it irritating but intriguing that God's campaign is often subtle and scaringly ambiguous about something so important for all of humanity. *Why not just make it plain speak and crank it up loud?* Rather, Jesus entices listeners to tune their listening to a different frequency. The kingdom of God can be easily drowned out and stepped over in our surge to be the church. We may pass by the tree everyday and it fades into the scenery, going unnoticed. But when we have eyes to see, we behold the Tree of Life budding up when previously overlooked. We see God's kingdom forestry. God's kingdom is being planted among us but

5. McLaren, *The Secret Message of Jesus,* 45.
6. Ibid., 46.

trees do not fight, they bear fruit. We are not coerced by the kingdom of God; we are not battered into submission and overwhelmed with the sheer sensory overload of its presentation. Rather the Tree invites us, intrigues us, and mystifies us. The creator of the world is gathering people together not to compete with the machinery of the world but to point out what is sprouting up unnoticed in this place. God is restoring relationships in creation, albeit in slow, subterranean, and subversive ways. God treasures this world like a gardener does her garden, tending to it, watering, weeding, and watching over it. And now Jesus' strategy is one of covert recruitment: "come labor with me to build a Tree of Life in your place." We must begin to look at every facet in light of this *kingdom Tree,* allowing it to loom over our present pursuits.

The tree as a metaphor for the kingdom of God may not scratch our itch for a blockbuster approach to cultivating a church for the future; this is the upside-down way of the kingdom. The Tree of Life speaks to an alternative future that does not revolve around the dynamo of personality, but rather the character of rootedness. The hotel is the icon of posing, posturing, and performing to establish a visibly secure identity; yet we are being summoned to a new way of being human, a submerged pattern for shaping an identity. "Identity" is that hard-to-quantify interior fabric that we feel makes us who we are, but we feel is perceptible by an audience of our preference. Our mind's eye has an emotional coliseum assembled, where we desperately hope our caricature is taken in with distinct features. It's what we want people to know us as. Hear this: our understanding of *how* the kingdom of God sprouts up in the world is directly related to the way in which we will seek out being visibly significant in the world as leaders.

PUMMELED BY NOISE

The church is in a precarious place, sitting atop the rubble of super-sized growth.[7] We've racked up a lot of wins. Whether you serve in a small or big church is not the issue. No matter the size of the church you lead or participate in, Western church leaders' imaginations and metrics for success are shaped by the most celebrated success stories. Our collective intelligence knows how to succeed at "church." This question of "how to be a successful church" has weighed heavy on me as a pastor for the last decade, knowing that beyond the phenomenon we've whipped up, God is cautioning us in 1

7. Fitch, *The Great Giveaway,* 121.

Samuel 16:7: "The LORD does not look at the things human beings look at. People look at the outward appearance, but the LORD looks at the heart."

In 1936, Adam Smith coined the phrase "unintended consequences"[8] to explain acts intended to cause a specific outcome that create other outcomes that are not the original one intended. There are unintended consequences for "best church practices" in our life together. Our razor-sharp leadership has unintentionally *severed* the palatable, rooted embodiment of the kingdom tree in our neighborhoods. Our well-organized approach to building a successful church has done damage to our bodies, like a hard-working miner now stuck with lungs ravaged by rock dust. We have done injury to our own roots.

Don DeLillo's novel *White Noise* portrays Jack Gladney, a successful professor. Jack's world is filled with achievements but is being unsettled by the bombardment of information and the hypocrisy in his own life. *White Noise* explores themes that were emerging during the late twentieth century, like rampant consumerism, media saturation, novelty academic intellectualism, the disintegration of relationships, and human-made disasters.[9] Jack is becoming more attuned to the noise always babbling in the background of his life. The first part of *White Noise*, called "Waves and Radiation," chronicles his contemporary family life that appears as a frenzy of activity, human detachment, and the surge of narcissism from the abundant availability of goods and services. Then suddenly a lethal black chemical cloud, an "airborne toxic event" unleashed by an industrial accident, floats over Jack's town. The airborne toxic event becomes symbolic of the white noise engulfing the Gladneys—the radio transmissions, sirens, microwaves, and TV murmurings that constitute the magic of American life. Jack at one point says in a satirical exclamation, "this is why people's eyes, ears, brains and nervous systems have grown weary, it's a simple case of being abused by noise."[10]

The church is living under an airborne toxic event created by the chaos of our own pragmatic, robust church noise. We have the residue of success on our hands but we are under a chemical cloud gasping for air, fresh air. There is a tactile quality that eludes us in the bone and marrow of our collective presence in the world. There is a way to be meaningful Jesus

---

8. University Discoveries, "Law of Unintended Consequences."

9. DeLillo, *White Noise*, 134.

10. Ibid, 94.

communities on God's earth that our "success" is not awakening. We are "winning" but we are tragically losing.

THE NUMBERS LEASH

We've heard the statistics about how the church in the West is fading fast. Every year denominations report they are hemorrhaging numerically. The category called the "Nones" is on the rise. In America, there are more than 13 million self-described atheists and agnostics, as well as nearly 33 million people who say they have no particular religious affiliation.[11] In my own city 96.5 percent of the city inhabitants do not attend church.[12] There are a million opportunities offered to the church that can spread its message wider, elevate its leaders higher, expand its budgets deeper, and grow its influence stronger. I sense it is a major misstep to address renewal in the church by starting with how to propagate it or prevent it from shrinking. Not once when addressing the seven churches in the book of Revelation does God mention numerical growth or the urgency of attracting more people. Honing our strategies for stimulating growth doesn't seem to be the concern of the New Testament letters. How many converts did the disciples make when Jesus sent them out on their first mission? We don't know. Matthew seems uninterested in this metric. We've allowed our fixes to be led around by the numbers leash. We are twisting and turning under the strain of numbers.[13] The unnerving truth is God gets heated when leaders survey the success of their organizations using numerical metrics. "David took a census of the people of Israel commissioning Joab to count the inhabitants of Israel. 'Take a census of all the people of Israel—from Beersheba in the south to Dan in the north—and bring me a report so I may know how many there are. But Joab replied . . . 'But why, my lord the king, do you want to do this?' The king insisted that they take the census, so Joab traveled throughout all Israel to count the people. . . . God was very displeased with the census. Then David said to God, 'I have sinned greatly by taking this census. Please forgive my guilt for doing this foolish thing'" (1 Chr 21:1–8).

We need to stop emphasizing the most obvious, simplistic cultural signs of success. Albert Einstein said, "That which counts is often the most

11. Pew Research Center, "Nones on the Rise."
12. Payne, "Least Churched Cities," 19.
13. White Jr., "The Numbers Leash."

difficult to count."[14] I've found this to be true. Numbers tell us very little about rootedness. Our location in a postindustrial, Western, efficiency-oriented economy has influenced our framework for ministry. We are conditioned to think in terms of verifiable, stock-market-type results, seeing churches like machines. We tweak this program and adjust that program, add some marketing, crunch the numbers, and produce results—a "if you do this, you get that" mentality. We need to snap the numbers leash. We need a fresh exploration into being the church that has little do with the numerical soap opera we all like to get caught up in. Rather, we have agricultural kingdom work to do, work that cares less about spreadsheets and more about getting rich soil and earth under our fingernails in our life together and in the life of our neighborhood. We need to confront our contemporary assumptions about what it means to be a significant church.

What assumptions about growth do we need to confront?

TEARING UP ROOTS

Years ago a friend of mine wanted to put up a garage in his backyard. I still don't know why he asked for my help since at that point I had a fear of power tools. I've learned how to swing a hammer since, but back then I felt like an Alaskan bobsledder in the ghettoes of Mexico. But I jumped in, uncertain if I'd do more harm than good. My friend had a computer-generated blueprint for constructing this two-car garage that included a small loft. He had been planning this garage for the last two years, saving up some money and meeting the appropriate town ordinances. When I arrived we started digging with a rented backhoe and went to town on a thirty-by-thirty-foot area. We roped out the section and were precise on how far down and wide we dug. A week later we poured the foundation with some help. We slaved in the hot sun and completed the first stage. We went through all the phases of framing, roofing, and electrical installation. Two months later we hung the metal garage door and had a completed garage. It wasn't my garage, but I took a lot of pride in that accomplishment. With great planning, lots of work, and the right tools we had built something to feel good about. A few years later at a party I had asked him a casual question about his garage. He reiterated that he loved it. It was wonderful during the snowy

14. Quoted in Garfield, *Peak Performance,* 112.

winters and he was also enjoying the loft for jamming with some musicians. He then stated with regret that a huge tree a few feet away from the garage was dying. It was a beautiful oak that his kids had climbed on and swung from. A source of great family memories was suddenly decaying. His hunch was that we had unintentionally extirpated its roots when we dug the garage's foundation. Roots are the principal organ for sustaining a tree. The roots anchor the tree's body, and can store reserve food. Roots usually grow beneath the surface of the soil and extend from the base of the trunk. Roots grow downward for stability, absorbing nutriments. Without a significant portion of its roots my friend's tree could not survive. In our effort to build an impressive structure we did damage to that beautiful tree. This is the exact predicament we find the church caught in. We have been planning the church, building the church, using the best tools to assemble the church—but we have unintentionally severed some vital, life-sustaining roots in the process. My premise is that we've excavated the very roots we need for anchorage of the in-breaking kingdom of God and nourishing life together in the world.

What roots have we unintentionally demolished?

This book is concerned with that nuance. Typically we think of nuance as a small, lesser, potentially insignificant conversation. The future of missional presence in the world will need a revival in our attention to nuance, which is, granted, the hardest thing to count. Rootedness probes around in the material of our character rather than in the clearer categories of what "works." Rootedness is less interested in the sheer utility of our outcomes and more interested in whether or not our practices humanize or dehumanize ourselves and others. Rootedness as I'm handling it gives resolute respect to what is occurring on a subterranean level.

2

Excessive Personality

THERE IS A QUESTION posed to us at an early age. It's a question that once given legs starts running after us, biting at our heels for the rest of our lives. Even if you answer this question as early as possible it will still chase you and then hide behind a corner. I remember having to draw a picture in third grade that reflected the answer to this important question: "What do you want to be when you grow up?" I have a complicated relationship with this question. I've always suspected this question is poking at more than a mere job choice. When I hear "What do you want to be when you grow up?" through my jaded lens I now hear "What good are you going to offer this world?" This question puts many on the stand in a psychological court, demanding we answer for our very existence. Obviously as a third grader I did not interact with this question though the lens of such anthropological cynicism. Being an excitable grade school kid in a public school, I was more than happy to oblige. Church syndrome was in my blood so I drew a picture of a pastor preaching from behind a pulpit. I stick-figured myself waiving my hands in exclamation, sporting a tie only a stick figure could wear. I drew a bubble over my sketched stick-head saying "God loves you . . ." From an early age I had this image of ministry that appeared larger than life, as an astronaut did for other children. The pastors of my youth were superstars to me. Listening to a booming voice, elevated on a stage, preaching the Word of God on a Sunday morning, made it nearly impossible to resist this powerful dynamic. The idea of being in ministry appeared exhilarating. I wish I could say that my desire to be a pastor was completely pure and shining with a holy polish. Sure, somewhere mixed in there was the eagerness to help and love people. But now that I know myself a little better than I did in third grade, I have a clue as to what my stronger motivations were. Something very elementary was hidden underneath my hopes of being a minister. I wanted to make a mark on the world, to have an impact. This was the base for my outlook on life. Somewhere I had an emotional wallet that when unfolded held an iconic picture of what "impact" looked like; it was visible, observable, and applaud-able. So in third grade I stretched for what I knew would make me compelling and memorable. The need for significance was a current pulsating through all my school years. I did not want to be a loser relegated to leftovers. Now I'm not exactly sure how being a "loser" would actualize itself—it was more of a blurry beast that haunted me. I couldn't really make it out or tell you the beast's name but I was frightened that I might be devoured. Most every endeavor I got involved with as a youngster was intertwined with this sense. The very things I loved were infused with an insidious longing to be significant.

We learn how the world works early on. Those that gather attention and stack up accomplishments are the envy of others; they are remembered while others are forgotten. They have crowds swarming around them when others don't. I'm convinced this observance lodged in my adolescent mind and affected much of my maneuvering for a long time.

In my early twenties at a small Christian college this inner paranoia about "losing" continued to coalesce. I was a passionate young man, climbing the ladder of the modern Christian life. Daily I rose early to pray, being so inspired by the testimonies of missionaries. I devoured every inspiring biography on the shelves of our college's mothball-smelling library. I was on a quest to mimic my spiritual heroes. I handwrote one hundred Scripture verses on three-by-five cards and carried them with me for the purpose of "hiding God's word in my heart." I attended a missions conference on campus in the mid-nineties with the theme "Impacting the World for Christ" printed in Comic Sans on a banner hung over the stage. I heard stories of missionaries and revivalists who did great things for God because they took great risks for God. The loud clarion call weighed heavily on my shoulders that week. *Did I want to make an impact for God?* I experienced palatable panic around that question. I couldn't really nail down a definition for "making an impact" but I knew how it felt in the form of a stress headache and some restless nights. At the end of that year my Christian college awarded me a scholarship. This was an award given to one student exhibiting outstanding Christian character. I remember strolling up on that stage feeling a surge of self-worth. I was the model of Christian achievement in the tiny world I resided in, yet I was drowning inside. I was caught in a serious cycle of insomnia brought on by stress. I was privately falling apart, missing work and frightening my wife as I became further depressed and detached. I visited a few doctors and sat with spiritual counselors; consoling words bounced off me. I had to "make an impact" so there was little space to listen. At twenty-two years of age I was experiencing a serious crisis. I wrestled all night every night, rehearsing over and over the challenges of the next day. I was an emotional hot mess, but at least I was significant in the eyes of others, right?

Eventually I was able to identify how my ambitions to be significant where whittling away at me. Still, twenty years after that college missions conference visions of "impact" attempt to pester me daily. I am petrified of being ordinary. My life is peppered with this theme. It's taken some uncomfortable examination to see that third grader and college student is still attempting to camp out inside me, keeping an anxiety fire flickering inside. I'm confessing: I want to make an impact and I want to measure that impact by external factors and voices. Maybe my inner world is repelling you but I've discovered I am not alone. I've met many pastors and parishioners who share in varying portions of this haunting. This anxiety is not quarantined to a leader's heart: it influences how we construct and design the church. When ministry plays into the game of competitive significance the result will be a pathological anxiety.

STATUS ANXIETY

Status anxiety is a term coined by Alain de Botton.[1] It is a nervous stress about our personal impact on the world. Status anxiety distorts what it means for us to be meaningful, memorable, and maximized. It is the convergence of factors that create an inner apocalypse around our perceptions of mattering in the world. It is a toxic paranoia that disfigures how we measure ourselves and gauge our footprint in society. Status anxiety has riddled us with all sorts of emotional turmoil. Forty million adults in the United States suffer from some sort of anxiety disorder. We spend $42 billion a year on dealing with these anxieties. Major Depressive Disorder is

---

1. Botton, *Status Anxiety,* 65–66.

the leading cause of disability in the US for those ages fifteen to thirty-five.[2] These stats may not be emotionally palatable to you but I can attest to the way they land in real-time ministries and in real-life leaders. Status anxiety terrorizes our egos. We are all utterly afraid of being ordinary. Status anxiety is constructed on the foundation of self-actualization. The highest value in the modern age is self-actualization. Psychologist Abraham Maslow became one of the pioneers behind the school of thought known as humanistic psychology in the mid-1950s. His crowning theory was the subject of self-actualization. In his banner book, *Toward a Psychology of Being*, Maslow laid out a hierarchy of needs starting with our basic needs of food and shelter and culminating in our ultimate need to self-actualize. More than observing, he was prescribing. According to Maslow the desire to reach one's greatest potential is the highest purpose of life, "To become everything that one is capable of becoming."[3]

He felt that once a person's deficiency needs (basic) were met they could turn all their attention to self-actualization. Maslow's classic summary of self-actualization was "what a man can be, he must be."[4] To him this unilateral self-actualizing pursuit was a sign of emotional health, even though he conceded that anxiety sustains the pursuit. Self-actualization has recently experienced a furious resurgence in popular Western thinking. I find a subtle pathology in Maslow's trajectory, one that perpetuates a nasty case of narcissism.

As a pastor, counselor, and a bit of an ad hoc sociologist for almost twenty years, I have seen a tidal wave in anxieties related to status. The opportunities for materializing our dreams have accelerated. New longings are being created because new opportunities are paraded before us. The more exposure we have to the achievements of others the more pressure we feel to actualize them for ourselves. Comparison is the reference point for self-actualization. We size up whether we should feel significant by looking at the misery or conquests of others. Facebook is a small sampling of the status anxiety running through our veins and through our churches. Facebook's addictive power is that it metrifies our status in the world; it tells us how important we are in comparison to others. Recently Benjamin Grosser developed a browser plug-in that removes the numbers from your

2. Costello, "Anxiety and Depression in America."
3. Maslow, *Toward a Psychology of Being*, 45–46.
4. Maslow, "A Theory of Human Motivation," 375.

Facebook page. Here's an example of how things are different before and after using it:

Like · Comment · Share · 12 hours ago · ⊕

👍 10 people like this.

🔁 3 shares

💬 View all 7 comments

Like · Comment · Share · recently · ⊕

👍 people like this.

🔁 shares

💬 View all comments

"We still get to see that there are comments, that people like the post and have shared it—and some sense of time. But there are no numbers. There are no 'key indicators.' Why is this important?" Grosser comments: "As a regular user of Facebook I continually find myself being enticed by its endless use of numbers. How many likes did my photos get today? What's my friend count? How much did people like my status? I focus on these quantifications, watching for the counts of responses rather than the responses themselves, or waiting for numbers of friend requests to appear rather than looking for meaningful connections. I believed the number told me something about myself, whether I was important that day."[5]

I'm not a runner but I wish I was. I've made a few attempts at the habit of pounding the pavement. Last summer I was able to run for about a month straight and was feeling pretty good about myself. Then one afternoon my euphoric feelings turned to embarrassment. I was running up a hill in our neighborhood when suddenly I heard the steps of another runner. This muscle-cut dude breezed past me. He even gave me a little glance and a smirk as he made it appear he was just riding an escalator. Immediately I felt like crumbs. I was given a comparison and now my bliss was banished. Our rapid self-actualizing does not happen in a vacuum. We are constantly pulled to define our contentment by the chorus of achievements around us.

5. Quoted in Brewin, "The Tyranny of Numbers."

CULTURE OF PERSONALITY

Twenty-five years later I still have apparitions from my morning routine standing in front of mirror fixing my hair as a gawky teenager. Early nineties flannel-shirt grunginess was overtaking the hairsprayed sheen of the eighties, so I had to make myself look a bit unkempt without looking like I was trying too hard. Every day I woke up I felt the pressure to be something special. Questions of significance framed that stare into the mirror. *As I walked through the halls would people notice me? Would I have anyone to sit with at lunch? Would that girl notice my new shirt? Would I embarrass myself in gym class?* My identity was under the constant accusation of not making the grade. Every adjustment I made to my appearance, every achievement made or not made, every compliment tossed in my general direction, was kindling wood for the fire I was laboring to keep alive—a fire of personality. *What would people see? How would they perceive me? Was I memorable? Was I important to my peers? Was there a place for me?*

These are vivid ghosts when you're a teenager, scaring the confidence out of you. These questions poked and prodded me. They demanded a sufficient response in my life. Because I weighed them so heavily they shaped my becoming. I jumped through personality hoops and ran through the obstacle course to make myself memorable in the world of my peers. The blunt noticeability of these questions changes as we grow up and get smarter at pretending. Yet many adults are still wrestling with this adolescent tossing and turning related to their significance and viability in the world. So we bend under their oppressive weight. The last thing we want to be is ordinary. This identity crisis is pandemic inside and outside the church. The selfie is one awkward signpost of our insecurity. We're frightened that people won't see us. Danny Bowman grew suicidal due to his addiction to taking selfies.[6] Bowman shared that he would shoot about 100 pictures a day in an attempt to take the "right" selfie of himself. He also said that he would spend hours editing selfies. Expert Pamela Rutledge explained in an article for *Psychology Today* that taking selfies is indicative of the tornado of narcissism. The selfie is the appropriate snapshot of the state of identity in the West. Paranoia that people don't see us, understand us, or find us essential is pushing, pushing, pushing self-expression to the center of our daily life.[7]

6. CBS Atlanta, "Selfie Addiction."
7. Rutledge, "Making Sense of Selfies."

How can we be a meaningful human in the world? That is the atomic question of our time, a question every individual is percolating on whether consciously or subconsciously. How we answer this question changes us. In Western culture, expression of preferences and inner feelings is considered the pinnacle achievement of freedom. Self-expression becomes core to how we define powerful individuality. This is called "expressive individualism."[8] To realize our identity, the road often laid out is increasing projection of one's thoughts and ideas into the world to ever-increasing acclaim. Through these self-expressive acts we are told that we'll become more recognizable and eventually apprehend that ever-elusive identity. Self-expression preaches that declaring our beliefs and opinions through bumper stickers, Twitter feeds, personal weblogs, or podcasted sermons will guide us to a more secure self. Self-expression has become the vehicle for identity formation. It is now a sacred act to self-express. This spiritual trajectory eventually leads to defining our personal identity in contrast to others, differentiating our uniqueness. Those same adolescent questions that caused me to glare into the mirror straining for ways to self-express have become enshrined in the cultural milieu of adulthood. Here is the consequence: thrusting our personality to the forefront as the core of identity formation unintentionally pushes the rooted work of responsibility to a neighborhood and long-term loyalty to community to the background of our ideas about identity formation. Independence, not interdependence, is the highest cultural value. What is ironic about this cultural doctrine of self-expression is that it's prescribed as the remedy for insecurity, which chronically perpetuates more insecurity. How we see being an *individually* significant personality parallels how we see being *collectively* significant. They are cross-pollinating conversations.

How does the church understand its personality? My own personal imagination for being extraordinary will influence and saturate what I believe makes an extraordinary church. They cannot be separated. How we want to be identified as significant in the world will directly influence how we want our churches to be applauded in the world. We'd like to think we can compartmentalize these two spheres but they work in tandem with each other in potent ways.

Historian Warren Susman coined the phrasing of a culture of character versus a culture of personality.[9] Susman shows that during the eighteenth

8. Bellah et al., *Habits of the Heart*, 78–79.
9. Susman, *Culture as History*, 96–99.

century a shift began to occur in American society. A new flavor started to sink in that pushed the tastiness of personality more than the substance of character. Rather than being concerned first with the state of *being* we became concerned with the state of *performing*. It's on this premise that self-expression founds its cathedral. What we began to count was not so much how one lived in the smallness of our towns but the impression one made in wider public opportunities. The pressure to impress took on its own virtue. Competition for status in a mobile world made how you "came across" of strategic importance more than any qualities you had quietly nurtured. The formation of personal significance paralleled the way the advertising world skirmished for identity.[10] A 1922 ad for Woodbury's soap warned, "All around you people are judging you silently," and the Williams Shaving Cream Company claimed, "Critical eyes are sizing you up right now." We began to tap into our entrepreneurial powers to achieve new heights, actualize brilliant ideas, and attain new levels of performance. For millennia the primary framework for identity was situated in interdependent communities. We would work together, often in the same town, needing each other for ordinary daily operations.[11] I don't want to romanticize that time period but I do want to point out that the Industrial Revolution began to flip that primary way of being significant. The rising emphasis fell on the *power of personality* to make things happen; captivating others with boldness, elegance, charm, intelligence, and entertainment became the tools for any individual or corporation that wanted to matter. The culture of personality is not only still with us but it is the smog that has been filling our sanctuaries and individual spirituality. The culture of personality aggressively shoves us to find more novel appearances to be the church, to test the limits of human potential. This cultural mandate to be spectacular is on overdrive. The extent to which the church became concerned with excellent presentations and dynamic personalities is unfortunate for our character.

The identity of the church is mixed up with this culture of personality. We have become known more for our personality fireworks than our quiet faithfulness, known more for our brands than for our humble presence. Since the church has taken this route of platforming its personality, the unassuming seedling of the kingdom tree has been stomped under our stampede for attention.

10. Cain, *Quiet*, 55–57.

11. Tickle, *The Great Emergence*, 45–46.

The future of the church needs to rebel against this culture of personality in order to pursue a culture of character. Certainly there is a "wow" factor in a church that can produce an appearance, but it is *rootedness* that gives our existence new possibilities in tangible kingdom ways. In the world of sparkle and spectacle, cleverness tries to charade as character. Character forged underneath the noise is what makes us who we really are.

GO BIG OR GO HOME

The typical heroes we now elevate, the gods of our time, are self-made individuals who achieve entrepreneurial magnificence off the draft of their personality. There is a cultural tsunami training us to collect and hoard esteem over and above our peers. The worship of impact is eerily related to the demigods in classical mythology. The term has been used in various ways at different times and can refer to a figure who has attained minor divine status, or a mortal who is the offspring of a god and a human. Julius Caesar was the first to be declared a demigod by the Roman Senate, after his victory at Thapsus in the first century BCE. The desire to become a demigod picked up momentum amongst commoners. It was surmised that to receive this status of demigod one would need either to perform a onetime astonishing act or gather affirmation and acclaim above all others in society. Adulation could be stockpiled, like a Klout score. Townspeople would begin to wonder if an exalted person was half human, half god. This demigod sentiment is alive and well today. The currency of our time is elevating oneself above our peers, reaching and stretching for a piece of the spotlight that will place our image in a godlike light.[12] We are squirming under the weight of apprehending and self-generating our image. The fuel for status anxiety is pumped into us daily through advertisements and the availability of comparisons through social media. The current trend is to guarantee our success by the fierce acquisition of it.

Our inner status anxiety has entangled itself in our church ambitions. We cannot separate our raging personal ambitions from the way many leaders and pastors *build* churches. Ambition claws, scrapes, and reaches for any reinforcements and tools. A large segment of Christianity's leaders are attempting to auto-tune the lyrics of power, ambition, and adulation and make them harmonize with biblical principles. Ambition mixed with status anxiety exasperates that weak spot in us to be significant in the

12. Carlyle, *Heroes*, 110–11.

world, finding fuel in those questions repeating in the prison of our minds: *How do we prove we have something essential to offer? How do we make something of ourselves? How can we matter? How can I have more influence, more leverage?* Our images of "significance" have been constructed more by the essences of Wall Street and Hollywood than spirit of the road to Damascus. Ambition and status anxiety knead upon as if we were dough, working their knuckles on our susceptible souls. This storm of pressure pushes the church towards *excessiveness*. Excessiveness in the church is propensity towards more and more esteem, exorbitant financial resources, an excitement of grand language, and insobriety in numerical growth. I contend that at the center of excessiveness is neurotic insecurity in the heart of leaders scrambling to build significant churches in the eyes of attendees, onlookers, and maybe even God.

An athletic coach at my high school had this mantra: bigger and stronger. He used to bark this slogan at us as he stormed through the weight room. I always hated that mantra because, well, I'm smaller, slower, and weaker. That mantra may work well in sports but I find it lethal in the church developing the character of presence. Ambition is often straining for leverage and an upper hand. Ambition places a memo in our mind's eye to look for the angle to catapult our ministry to the next level of production. The cyclone of the entire West is heading in the direction that bigger is better and smaller is boring. The most-readily trumpeted tools in the church are ones that increase the mass of our production. I actually met a guy who thought "go big or go home" was a verse in the Bible. Sadly and regularly the accomplishment of our ambitions overrules rootedness. Our big ambitions can condition us to use people as buffers to bounce off as we move toward our grand goals.

We must be careful to not baptize the concept of "accomplishing our dreams" and self-actualization in faith language. There is very little discipleship in the New Testament related to cultivating a personalized audacious vision to be authentically Christian. It's just not in there. The way we shortcut around this is to over-spiritualize, convincing ourselves and others that the fruition of our big dreams are good for the world and good for God. We are skilled at dressing up our ambitions in grand spiritual clichés that camouflage our status anxiety. In our good intentions to be someone and build something, venom is simultaneously sneaking into our bloodstream, riddling our bodies with a hunger for the bigger and stronger and distaste for the slower and smaller. Growth is often confused with expansion. In a culture that worships "big," getting bigger may not be a by-product of kingdom growth. Our culture slips us all kinds of shortcuts to pursue size through the use of marketing, money, and manipulative strategies that we often couch in faith language. When we take these shortcuts it is like an athlete taking the steroid route to building muscle. Bigness does boost our self-esteem, ushering in a wonderful feeling that what we're doing matters. The pursuit of bigness causes us to be blinded by grandiose infrastructure and fall victim to personality centrism. Leaders within big churches often are not egomaniacs but bigness creates a culture not hospitable to the smallness of incarnation. Many well-meaning leaders are in the business of empire building without even knowing it.

FRAGILITY OF PRESENCE

Recently my wife and I have been noticing and working out something with my nine-year-old boy. He is a human container of vivacious laughter, tantrums of creative brilliance, quirky commentary, and strong moral sensitivities. He's an absolute joy and amusement when you spend time with him. Daydreams swirl around in his head. He knows how to play to the point of exhaustion. Just recently someone from our community popped into our house unexpectedly to say hello. They have kids about my son's age. At the same time they came over, my son was racing through the living room looking for a lost Lego that he wanted to add to the tower he was building in his bedroom. He had to find this missing piece for his visionary project. When my boy starts working on a creative venture with Legos he gets in the zone. So as this family walked into our living room to say hello my son blew right past them without the slightest nod. He was on a mission and these people were not part of it. I watched as their little girl looked up at her mom with concerned panic in her eyes, as if to say "Does Daniel not want to play with me?" One of the things we've noticed is how his personal ambition can cause him to give people a cursory acknowledgment. Late that night as I was singing him a song and tucking him into bed, I asked why he ignored his friend earlier in the day. He said "Dad, I didn't ignore her, I just had big stuff to do." His big stuff was more important than people. I've committed this crime so many times myself. My ambition seeks to push past being present with others. I began to reflect on how many times over the years my inner voice said "I'm not ignoring people, I've just got big stuff to do."

The kernel of presence is fragile, easily crushed by the big footprint of our ambitions. The space and stillness required to be present with people is always under duress from our ardent undertakings. When it comes to being the church I find nothing more easily snuffed out than the availability, touchability, vulnerability, and responsibility critical for human presence. Presence in not just a "personal" thing, it is the very way the society of the church is to be identified and constituted. Presence is where the kingdom of God touches human existence. Efficiency is a terrible replacement for presence. Near Decapolis, some people brought Jesus a man who could hardly talk. Jesus healed the man in a curious manner: "Jesus put his fingers into the man's ears. Then he spit and touched the man's tongue" (Mark 7:33). Jesus also healed a blind man on another occasion: "He spit on the man's eyes and put his hands on him" (Mark 8:23). To heal another man Jesus "spit on the ground, made some mud with the saliva, and put it on the man's eyes" (John 9:6). Certainly, Jesus did not need physical props. So this was an odd way to extend healing, don't you think? Have you ever tried making some mud with your own saliva? I'm sure Jesus needed multiple spittles to make mud. In each case he rubs his fingers on people, mixed with his own bodily fluid. Today we'd be freaking out and telling him to put latex gloves on. Jesus, God in the flesh, deliberately chooses means that are menial and exceptionally human. Instead of an elaborate polished ceremony the kingdom comes in simple, unsanitary, messy ways—perhaps even indecent ways. Jesus uses his own spit and the dirt at his feet to connect the mysteries of the kingdom of God to people. The kingdom does not overwhelm us in a spectacle of sight and sounds—rather it will dwell with us in unsettling ordinariness. Jesus doesn't make any practical sense in an economy of power, prestige, and production. Our aversion to anything mediocre and ordinary comes more from our culture of personality. To be subterranean we must ask hard questions about what ambitious assembling, and constructing *without* strong discretion, does to the fragile flicker of presence—being with, really with, people.

What have our ambitions done to the church's ability to be present in the world?

Move Along Jesus

The Gospels emphasize that the Father has sent Jesus as one of us. God does not scorn the human condition; instead, God dwelt in the fragility of the human body (Phil 2). This human form brought the glory of God down from Mt. Sinai to the streets of Nazareth, closing the relational fault line. The fullness of God somehow, some way was displayed in the limitations of the God-man Jesus. He embraced those limits to model for us how to be present to humanity. Jesus was a "manger wetter" as the poet Stephen Mahan states.[13] This is not sacrilegious, this is sacred. Jesus the Messiah moved into the Nazareth neighborhood for thirty years and few recognized his identity. He was a good kid, employee, and participant in his community long before his ministry went public. Really, God went subterranean. *Would we be okay with laying low like this?* The closest parallel I can muster is if President Obama grew a bushy beard, let his hair go all gray and moved into an apartment on your street. He mowed his own lawn, babysat the neighbor's kids, and hosted barbeques. Few, however, had a clue it was the commander in chief chilling on their block for three decades. That is a wild proposition, but the fullness of God hid out in the body of the blue-collar carpenter Jesus. Jesus is the perfect Word of God in the container of a human life. God experienced human flesh and in it opened up space to observe the loving-kindness of the Godhead (Rom 2:4). The incarnation continues as he was sent (John 20:21) and now the divine is being downloaded into the ordinary. An incarnational God leads us to inhabit the world not as one fearing but as one searching; searching how the kingdom of God breaks into the crevices of our world through intentional presence.[14] Jesus' love was squeezed through the wringer of a neighborhood. This imagination is a burst of light into my life, offering me an impetus for being in my local context. Yet the incarnation confronts our ambitious leadership. How will we be present? The theology of presence lifts off the page in the vivid interaction between Jesus with the hemorrhaging woman. "In the crowd that day there was a woman afflicted with hemorrhages. . . . She slipped in from behind and touched the edge of Jesus' robe. At that very moment her hemorrhaging stopped. Jesus said, 'Who touched me?' When no one stepped forward, Peter said, 'But Master, we've got crowds of people on our hands. Dozens have touched you.' . . . When the woman realized that

---

13. Russ, *Flesh and Blood Jesus*, 45–46.

14. White Jr., "Irritation of Incarnation."

she couldn't remain hidden, she knelt trembling before him. In front of all the people, she blurted out her story—why she touched him. Jesus said, 'Daughter, you took a risk trusting me, and now you're healed and whole. Live well, be a blessing!'" (Mark 5:25–34.) This interaction is overwhelming, a picture of the cosmic creator crashing into human bleeding; this is the gospel of the kingdom and its burgeoning arrival. Notice the interruption of ambition. I see myself in Peter. *"Let's move along Jesus, come on, we've got stuff to get to, we've got a cause we're on, we're building a revolution here."* The disciples are miffed by Jesus' inefficiency. The Son of God does not see presence with people as an impediment. I am sometimes struck by thoughts of the hundreds of lepers Jesus did not heal, the thousands of people he did not feed. Jesus healed so few.[15] Our ambitions will try to push us from behind to blow past the smallness of the kingdom of God. My strong suspicion is that we no longer have ears to hear and eyes to see *how* the kingdom materializes. Our binoculars are honed for one thing on the horizon: bigger, better, bolder. Our concepts of leadership are thoroughly dipped in the syrup of celebrity, the political process, and performance as influence. There is horsepower in the engine of the modern church that thrusts us toward the ramp of success. I've wanted my own church to be successful but presence must be allowed to bother us, put up a roadblock and change the way we construct the way we do church. We must embrace contours of resistance to our ambitions.

The etymology of the word *ambition* in Middle English is *ambicion*, which means "excessive desire for honor, power, or acclaim." Ambition is used differently today to speak of being active or being a go-getter, yet ambition plays hide-and-go-seek with what drives it. It cloaks itself in sentiments that seem altruistic, but many well-meaning leaders have desires to *conquer* that appear on the surface as innocently passionate. "Ambition is a hunger; it obeys no law but its appetite," said humorist Josh Billings.[16] Ambition is sly as it convinces us that our success is good for others, so it propels us to self-promote for the benefit of God and his glory. It only takes a shred of immaturity for ambition to percolate insatiable desires in the soul that are willing to add small portions of competition, coveting, envy, aggression, manipulative control, and enemy identification. Few leaders begin with these dark drives but the pursuit of accruing success makes our adolescent insecurities susceptible to corruption. Ambition opens

15. Paul, *God in the Alley,* 78–79.
16. Billings, *Complete Works,* 129–30.

us up to the use of excessive techniques to secure victory. Consider the scriptural narrative exposing when ambition starts to creep in: Adam and Eve responding to the tempter saying "you will be like God" (Gen 3:5) or the gathered people saying, "Come, let us build a city, with a tower that stretches to the heavens, so that we may create a name for ourselves" (Gen 11:4) or the disciples asking Jesus to sit next to him in the kingdom (Mark 10:35–40). We want to be the main character, the celebrated, the superhero, the face on the screen.

Ambition has become baptized in Christian best-seller land. The neglected little book of Jude warns against leaders who are driven by ambition, leading them into all sorts of foolishness. Jude counsels us with some fire to discern self-control that avoids the spiraling destruction that unhindered ambition brings. He compares leaders who give in to their ambition to the "the angels who did not keep their positions of authority but abandoned their proper dwelling—these he has kept in darkness, bound with everlasting chains for judgment on the great Day" (v. 6). Jude is interpreting Genesis 6, which sees the "sons of God" as cosmic rulers that took on bodies in order to have sexual relations with humans, and spawned a race of giants. Jude doesn't refer to these figures to fascinate modern readers, but to point out for churches that leaders who do not control their ambitions are in danger, like those cosmic figures. He warns that such leaders are captive to their own ambitions. "They boast about themselves and flatter others for their own advantage . . . . They follow mere natural instincts and do not have the Spirit" (vv. 16–19). Leaders often receive praise for their ambition and impressive strategies; yet in the church this type of leadership is a tightrope walk, rife with peril.

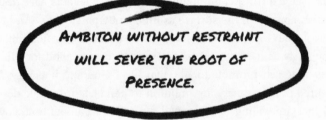

AMBITON WITHOUT RESTRAINT WILL SEVER THE ROOT OF PRESENCE.

SENSATIONALISM

The excessive impulse within the church gravitates to methods that will export its brand, accessorize its programs, and expand its footprint. The easiest way to stimulate energy around a big agenda is to tap into the electric power of communication. Sensationalism is a social communication force maneuvering to convince us "that if you are not sensational you will not be heard and then you will not be important." Since the term *sensationalism* was coined in the late 1800s this sentiment has been slowly taking over communication and presentation. Sensationalism is a type of editorial approach in media in which events and topics in news stories are hyped to increase viewership or readership. This type of communication understands something intuitively: if you can spark a sensation you can be the source to define reality. In the mid-1890s William Hearst was the publisher of the *New York Journal,* battling for newspaper readers.[17] His competition was Joseph Pulitzer, who published the *New York World.* In February of 1898 an explosion sank the USS Maine, killing 266 men. The American battleship was in the harbor of Cuba. The cause could have been an accident or a Spanish mine, but the public—including Hearst's and Pulitzer's newspapers—quickly blamed Spanish forces. Soon after, the US declared war on Spain. As the war raged, Hearst bragged to readers, "How do you like the *Journal's* war?"[18] Both Hearst and Pulitzer discovered the power of sensational headlines. Both papers made events seem more exciting than they really were. The benefit was that each paper sold almost a million copies a day. This is called the era of yellow journalism. Sensationalism was designed to produce a strong reaction—anger, disgust, exhilaration, etc. To be sensational is to manufacture excitement, to create intrigue that breeds attraction. The quality of something is measured by how it encounters our senses, creating a cultural doctrine that ascribes importance to something by the gratification it offers us immediately. The pleasure or lack of pleasure that our senses are offered become our primary barometer for ascribing value, training us how to determine worth; invisibility has become intolerable. It is borderline necessary for survival in the world of business, communication, and media as it bludgeons us with crafty language. This approach to communication is rampant in media but has sadly spilled uncritically into the DNA of the Western church. The steady diet of the parade of "wow" in our culture has progressively shaped how we posture the church in our society. Sensationalism appears in subtle statements about why "our church has great (fill in the blank) that no other church has." This is ruinous to the character of the church, yet it's become commonplace and unquestioned. We bow to the measuring stick of whether something inspires us to merit our faithfulness.

17. Skog, *Yellow Journalism,* 15–16.
18. Ibid., 22.

What seems ordinary is unimportant and less value is placed on it. So the temptation is to exaggerate the ordinary in order to make it extraordinary. Too many churches buy into these behaviors of communication, declaring "God's doing something" before he's doing something. When our communication no longer seeks to be grounded but to soar high in competitive air space we are destined to lose *presence*. The gospel of the kingdom does not call us to produce wows each week. We must rebel against being mesmerized by the veneer of sensationalism. The Apostle Paul shares his own resistance to sensationalism when says to the church in Corinth: "You'll remember, friends, that when I first came to you to declare the testimony of God's work, I did not try to impress you with polished speeches and eloquence. I deliberately kept it plain: who Jesus is and what he did—Jesus crucified. I came to you in weakness, feeling inadequate, if you want the truth of it I was unimpressive. But it was God's Spirit that made the message clear to you. I did not want your faith to rest on fancy mental or emotional tactics—only on the truth of the Gospel" (1 Cor 2:1–5).

MARKETPLACE SENSIBILITIES

I recently had to find a car since my old one croaked. So I began running through the shopping gauntlet to find a used car dealer that had what I was looking for. I started with places that I knew of. I admit it; I started with dealerships that air those obnoxious screaming commercials offering deals. Locally we have a dealer that screams in a smoker's voice at the end of every commercial "It's HUGE." I've heard that slogan so many times on local radio that it's jimmied its way into my cortex. The commercial was riddled with small exaggerations and assertions that few would inspect. So I'm a bit embarrassed to admit it lured me in when I began my car-hunting expedition. I couldn't resist the potential of getting a good car for a cheap price with no down payment. I was drawn in like a fly to an outdoor barbeque. I didn't end up buying a car from the "HUGE" dealership. Yet something about that occurrence unsettled me somewhat. I know it's completely normal in the consumer economy to buy based on the deals a seller can offer. Still, I don't like that the circus of noise was able to enrapture me, sway my mind, and potentially sway my decisions. In the competition to sell cars, obviously the marketing consensus is the noisier the claims, the more memorable. Well, it worked—I remembered them. This thrust "to be remembered" has become a rule by which most entities live and die. I think I can understand this when dollars are on the line. Still, I'd make a crummy millionaire because I value realness over revenue. Either way, for as much of a purist as I'd like to think I am, in my veins runs a hunger for more. I'm drawn in by whatever gleams and glams on the horizon of choices. In many ways this drive is on stealth mode in my subconscious but attempts to influence many of my overt choices. My emotions, my wants, my desperations, my demands, are used as an advantage against me. These felt needs whisper that they must, *must* be gratified. They are a hidden apparatus leveraging attention, seeking excess to be content. In the cultural imagination, a "good" church is one that meets the majority of my needs. If you want a significant church give people what they want. In fact, you may end up with something culturally impressive but you won't have a church.[19] The demand for more, the insidious slide towards excess is severing the church from its rooted presence. No matter the worship style, creed, or color, sensationalism and marketplace sensibilities have become a conventional rubric for architecting our churches. The entertainment industry has squeezed between the lines of our liturgy. We're not representing a genuine alternative to the dominant culture when we use the dominant culture's tactics for production. The sly nature of excessiveness is a subliminal acceptance that *more* is inherently a good moral. The church grows not by the majesty of its presentations but by the manifestation of its presence with each other, with the neighborhood, with the world.

The incarnational presence of Jesus is at stake when the tentacles of *excess* creep into our churches. Presence is under siege and it is fragile like a flower. It reminds me of the bad habit I have when I mow my lawn. I go into a bit of a tirade whacking everything in sight. In my hurry, in my blaze of grass-cutting madness, I've cut down flowers my wife gently and meticulously nurtured. Often the most beautiful realities are delicate and easily massacred. That's what makes them so beautiful in the harsh elements of the world. Presence is very much like this. We can declare the glory of God all day long, build worship sets that create sensory overload, assemble liturgical services that stimulate the mind, and preach sermons that peel the paint off walls, but *not* have presence. The social force of excess pummels presence in real ways. The last thing that the enemy of this world wants is God *with* us.

19. Fitch, *The Great Giveaway*, 112–14.

MISSIONAL MINIMALISM

In my first ten years as a pastor I became accustomed to resources. I worshiped and served with a charitable portion of resources as unidentified supports around me. I had great worship facilities, great budgets, and decently funded programs to suit any need or stage of life. I had on-hand artists to paint canvases for my sermons and quality writers to produce freshly written liturgies. I had talented musicians to create any mood we needed. Whenever I would start a new sermon series or spiritual program, I quickly found myself pondering what resources were needed to land it with excellence. I was convinced change happened from a sanctuary platform. Then one summer I went to Kenya and returned with hard questions pummeling my mind. In Kenya, I observed the fallout atrocities from tribal wars, unique farming methods in poor villages, and children who just wanted to play until the sun went down. Yet, there was something else that lodged under my rib cage: a one-hour conversation with a middle-aged Kenyan pastor. One afternoon this pastor took me on a village walk and then we moseyed into his hut for what he called a "pastor-to-pastor chat." I was expecting a delightfully rich spiritual conversation but I received a gentle yet pointed rebuke on American Christianity. The classic memorable line from my new prophet-pastor-friend was "we don't want your overstuffed Jesus." Ouch. He talked intensely about how buildings, budgets, and bands had crowded out the spirit of the church. With grace, he expressed how Jesus-followers in his own village gathered simply and cared for each other in their poverty and mission was extended through generosity to other villages. I was confronted and undone. God took me on a voyage after that conversation. My privilege had blinded me to the wisdom and splendor of minimalism. The term *minimalism* was coined right after World War II. It refers to a shift, found both in jazz and art, that pares everything down to the basics. It was a corrective needed to recover simple palettes. The term refers to something that is stripped to essentials, decluttering in order to craft *open* space. The end purpose is not open space. The open space provides more intentional focus on the inhabitants and their relation to each other. Minimalism, to quote William Henry Channing, seeks "to live content with small means."[20] As Nicholas Burroughs put it, "Minimalism is not a lack of something. It's simply the perfect amount of something."[21] Persecution or poverty typically

---

20. Channing, *The Spirit of the Age*, 160–61.
21. Burroughs, "Perpetuating Thought."

impose minimalism, but we need to embrace it voluntarily. Minimalism makes space for presence. We unknowingly relate through so many buffers. Minimalism reminds us to audit them.

Our churches have been held hostage by our grab for significance and status; we must subvert this quest. A church that does not seek to frustrate being excessive loses its quality of presence, of being with people. Presence requires a measure of resistance to our driving ambitions, our addiction to sensationalism, our marketplace sensibilities, and our tendency to dress up our Sunday gatherings. We need an exorcism to rid our apparitions related to being bigger and bolder. We will unpack praxis of presence in a future chapter on "Practicing Locality."

How can we restructure for presence? In our neighborhoods? With each other?

If the kingdom of God is like a tree sprouting up *above* the ground then we must ask what roots are plummeting *below* the ground. "The Kingdom of God is like a mustard seed that someone took and sowed in his garden; it is the smallest of all the seeds, but when it has grown it is the greatest of shrubs and becomes a tree, so that the birds of the air come and make nests in its branches" (Matt 13:31–32). The mustard seed is very small. When the gardener plants the seed, they expect little more than a shrub. Jesus is alluding to Ezekiel 17 when God compares the kingdom to the cuttings from a cedar tree that God plants. Seedlings from that tree grow into a expansive tree that all the birds come and make nests in. This kingdom tree, Jesus says, is a home for the birds of the air. This parable describes the tree as a shelter for all the birds of the air. This type of shelter is not created with our best ministry artillery and most exciting ministry personalities. There is something untraditional and unsettling about the agronomy that God's kingdom favors. There is a mysterious interplay between the subterranean roots the church cultivates and the expression of a life-giving kingdom tree. There is no tree without roots. We must wake up to a better way of being the church that is more about anchoring our souls than accruing a status. Jesus compared his work in the world to the most microscopic seeds, like the mustard seed. The future of the church needs a renewed imagination for the sacred smallness of presence as a means for the how the kingdom of God breaks in.

3

Extracted Perception

IN THE 1982 FANTASY film *The Dark Crystal*, Jim Henson's master puppetry goes gothic and dark. My wife watched *The Dark Crystal* as a kid and freaked out when she discovered I hadn't seen it yet. I'm a closeted sci-fi nut so I made it a movie night as soon as possible. In the film, the evil race of Skeksis are a fictional species that are part reptile, part predatory bird, part dragon, and rule their fantastical planet with an iron claw. One thousand years ago the mysterious dark crystal was damaged and an age of chaos began.[1] The Skeksis have possession of a piece of the dark crystal. Meanwhile orphan Podling Jen, raised in solitude by a race of peace-loving wizards called the Mystics, embarks on a quest to find the missing shard of the dark crystal, which gives the Skeksis their power, in order to restore the balance of the universe. Due to the accelerated decomposition of their bodies, the Skeksis are constantly searching for ways to prolong their lives. The Skeksis seek out life for the sake of adding to their own existence. They do this through a process of *extracting* vital essence from Podlings. The Skeksis use the beams of the dark crystal to extract life essence and are then able to fortify themselves. This process of *extraction* drains the victims of their spirit but keeps them barely alive. The process of extraction pulls an object of value to the surface but often leaves an object damaged in the process. The Skeksis try to get at the *essence* through extraction but must harm some element of life to continue their mission. Extraction is the process of getting

1. Henson and Oz, *The Dark Crystal*.

at a substance by removing it or separating it. In our own day and setting, this is the critique often leveled at fracking.

Fracking is a form of gas extraction. In the old days, a well was drilled straight down and gas was pumped up. Now, to get at less-accessible gas, wells are drilled thousands of feet down and then thousands more horizontally. Hydraulic fracturing pumps thousands of gallons of water, sand, and chemicals down the well to fracture the rock that holds the gas.[2] This extraction process boosts production, migrating natural gas, petroleum, and brine to the well. For all that is gained in fracking there is a growing chorus of people exposing the environmental impact that hydraulic fracturing has. Ground water is contaminated, air quality is ruined, and methane emissions make people sick. Few contest how productive fracking is for extracting gas. What is being contested is that the process leaves behind damage. Whatever your opinions on fracking are, they are irrelevant to what I'm poking at. The greater question I want to ask is "What does extraction do? What are the unintended consequences?" Often our celebration of extraction revolves around what is gained, pulled to the surface. Extraction always profits something, yet leaves behind something in the aftermath.

INFORMATION-INTAKE

Extraction leaves something damaged in the technique. I contend that the church has submitted to a technique that extracts. How we teach is *stuck* in a habit that enables extraction. In order to get at, isolate, codify, and distribute spiritual information we're damaging something in the process. The very way we execute the majority of our learning within the church through the vehicles of sermons, Sunday schools, six-week courses, and Bible studies often bolsters extraction. As with the Skeksis from *The Dark Crystal*, our mechanisms for delivering truth leave behind the character of *practice*, lifeless and inept. As with fracking, we may efficiently lift information to the surface but do environmental harm to our social existence as the church. Our current unquestioned approaches to transferring spiritual information are brutal on the virtue of practice. Practice is the inner quality of being formed and informed by the bumps, bruises, and baptism of application. Practice is at the soul of being a Jesus-follower but more so it becomes the material for credibility as the people of God. "But be people who live out the truth, not people who merely receive it and fool themselves.

2. Goldman, "Hydraulic Fracturing 101."

When you do this you are like a person who looks in the mirror, walks away, and then forgets what they look like" (Jas 1:22). Preaching harder and louder at people to practice what they hear will not resolve this issue; this is not an issue of volume. For the future of the church must recalibrate *how* we learn, understanding that we are *shaped* by the techniques we employ. The methods we implement for maturing as Jesus-followers either lead to increasing integrity in our practice or lead to an increasing inauthenticity in our practice. The actuality of practice, the material of our being and doing, is influenced absolutely by the ongoing learning habits we employ. The crisis with Evangelicalism's personality in the world is linked to credibility; an observable, palpable life in our local places. Very little of the future *health* of the church will depend on who has the corner on the best version of truth or who can disseminate information most efficiently. What matters, what is felt, what is dynamite is *what is truly practiced.* Practice is the character quality of being formed and informed by the application itself. To be subterranean is to descend deeper, seeking practice. There is a formula that has gradually crept into our spiritual imagination that looks like this:

More Information = Transformation

This has become a learning equation embedded in our church DNA. Our society believes that the imbibing of information equals change. Notice that the formula doesn't say:

Information + Immersion = Transformation

We often extract *information* from *immersion* in the process of learning. Do we really learn outside of immersion? When I say "immersion" I specify a full-bodied participation and practice in the information we encounter.

HABITS OF DISCIPLESHIP

When it comes to education, theology, and personal betterment, more and more of our learning processes perpetuate extraction, removal from habitation, in order to acquire the desired information. We've become accustomed to the gigantic separation between information intake and the simultaneous immersion. In many ways our higher education system models this dynamic. The merry-go-round often goes like this: young people ship off to school for four to six years to study specialized information only to be shocked and sometimes depressed once they score a job in their studied field, discovering they don't really like it all, or find it only bearable week in and week out after thousands of dollars spent on education. This occurs as a result of separation. In studying, students barely encounter the real-time reality in their academic rigors. There is a buffer that keeps them from learning by way of immersion. There are very few opportunities to learn from the ground up rather than top-down in a lecture hall. This is extraction, this is separation. We remove people in order to teach and train people. I have no intention of suggesting how to overhaul our education system. What I want to unfold is how the cultural norm for learning influences the church.

Divorcing *information* from *immersion* is something I bump into regularly. One can become an expert without immersed practice. It is all around us but we're acculturated to it. A few years back my wife and I went through a three-month adoption training course to get our adoption qualifications. I was taken aback when I asked our certified instructor his experience about a very specific family challenge that went beyond the written training material. His reply was, "I've never had a child in my home, not sure I'm cut out for that." Now I'm cool with his choice not to having children, but it was hard for my wife and I not to wince. Why wasn't this odd to anyone else? How can one be an expert in family therapy without ever being tested by the real-life challenges? I was studying under a credentialed expert who never touched and grappled with the information in the real world. This has become the norm rather than the exception. Can we know what is good, helpful, and true without swimming in a context that demands we flesh it out? It has become permissible to separate the information we store up *from* actualizing it. This used to be called hypocrisy, but now it's simply the way that we carry around (and sometimes sling around the information) we've collected in our mental folders. We can be proclaimed experts without immersion.

EXPERT DELUSION

There are many forces that *extract* us, working to keep us from embodying our values in a real place with real people. It seems like never before we are more inflamed or convinced about some theology, new idea, or cause that is less sourced from what is happening on the ground in our local places and more based on what provocative story we read online, what blog we recently devoured, or what podcast we just inhaled. So much of what grows hot in our heads does not come from kissing the pavement. We are fascinated with what we can discover that will boost our enlightenment or boil our blood. At times I'm lured into the lie that I can be an expert on something because I've taken in information on a specific matter. Peter Senge, in his book *The Fifth Discipline*, unpacks our fixation on becoming experts: "Being an expert gives us power and prosperity over our peers."[3] We secure our strength in our societal cosmos when we have more accumulated intelligence in our head than anyone else. This knowledge offers an expert delusion that we are not vulnerable to making the unenlightened errors others will. We fear ignorance; ignorance is our enemy. In no previous time has there been such a keg-like binging on information. We are rabid about acquiring information, but at what cost? A great divorce has been filed between information and immersion. This separation propels the opinionated milieu we find ourselves in and presumes we're better off because we're informed.

PRINCETON STUDY

At the recent Harvard Initiative for Learning, Jennifer L. Roberts, professor of humanities, has been reflecting on the ivory tower of teaching. "Although I use a broad digital technology in teaching, more and more I feel it is essential to give students experience in modes of attentive immersion that run directly counter to the high-speed, technologically assisted pedagogies emerging in this era. During the past few years, I have begun to feel that I need to take a more active role in personally shaping their experiences . . . . I still select readings, choose topics, and organize the sequence of material, but I'm wrestling with how to submerge them in formation and contemplation not just information."[4]

Extraction always has a victim; one of those victims is self-awareness. When learning happens in ways that extract us we lose self-understanding in what we actually do, what we practice daily. We live in our heads, convinced we are who we imagine we are. Environments that separate information from immersion cannot offer the mirror of self-awareness. Extracted learning reinforces the insulated self. A few years back my wife and I had launched our first garden in our backyard. I was a rookie in the domain

3. Senge, *The Fifth Discipline*, 130–31.
4. Roberts, "The Power of Patience."

of soil and seed. I had not grown up around farming. So we were eager to learn. I remember being at a party and sharing with a guest that we were beginning some agricultural craziness in our backyard. The well-meaning guy began to unload his expertise about what to do and not to do. I shared with him something we were doing and he passionately lectured back. Suddenly his wife walked up with a smirk on her face and said, "Honey, are you preaching about gardening again? Our own garden isn't doing so hot." I eventually found out this was his first garden, but he was convinced he knew most everything because he had an subscription to *Fine Gardening* magazine. His extracted learning developed poor self-awareness. He was not a very good gardener but was convinced he was because he had taken in info. We see this often within the church subculture. Preachers pontificate about the guilt-inducing importance of a "quiet time" under the projected notion of their successful habits, when in reality they are hit or miss themselves. I am not anti-information, but the way we ingest information has subtle but serious consequences on our lack of depth, integrity, and character. The more extracted the *self* that takes in information, the more projection will be on the rise. Psychological projection is the act of denying the existence of a negative impulses within oneself while attributing them to others.[5] Projection tends to hold a "group" to a standard they themselves are not personally able to live up to. Instead of dealing with our own character, we place our angst on a group. We find ways to unload without having to face ourselves in the mirror. Projection looks like being a staunch political fiscal conservative but sitting on $30,000 in personal credit card debt or being a staunch progressive advocating for human rights but showing little sacrificial compassion for one's next door neighbors.

I personally have always struggled with retaining information. I have a medium affliction of ADHD and a learning disability that haunted me throughout school. I was reminded daily how slow I was by the consistent C's and D's I pulled even after studying at all hours. Privately I hated myself for not being "smart." To this day I feel a swelling intimidation when I perceive how highly educated someone is. So I'm tempted to pour myself into buoying my brains to convince myself I'm catching up with the others above me on the academic hierarchy. It's easy to be deceived into believing that "the more I know the more I am." I meet many voracious readers with a desire to be brilliant that is often stronger than their desire to practice. We tremble at the thought of being stuck on the tarmac because we know less

5. Haber and Runyon, *Fundamentals of Psychology,* 230–33.

than the peers we compare ourselves to. This type of thinking lures us into a learning formula that cultivates duplicity. The separation between information and immersion has sundered our rootedness as the people of God. We've permitted our speech to wander far beyond what we exercise in actuality. There is a widening chasm between information and immersion, and the church has patterned its learning processes after extraction. This split between information and immersion has impoverished us, draining us and severing our rootedness in practice. May I suggest a potentially simplistic view of the conundrum?

INFORMATION WITHOUT
IMMERSION WILL SEVER THE
ROOT OF PRACTICE

OUR HISTORY OF LEARNING

The primary impetus for divorcing information from immersion is efficiency. Efficiency is often a response to an immediate concern. Plainly, it's just quicker and easier; it's productive. Immersion, a full-bodied practice within relationship and reflection, slows things down and messes things up. Programs often shield us from direct contact with people. It's this direct contact that can plug our efficient learning pipelines. So within this framework of efficiency it seems perfectly appropriate to eliminate the plug. We remove the clunky channels of relationship and long slow work of binding to one another. Remember Princess Leia's hologram to Obi Wan Kenobi in *Star Wars*? Eastlake Church in Washington has begun using holographic technology in their weekend services in multiple locations.[6] Kevin Olin, who installed the system at Eastlake, feels that it's hard to tell the difference between the live person on stage and the hologram. "I've watched the reaction of first time guests, many of whom don't even realize it's a video until maybe ten minutes into preaching." This might seem simply obnoxious, but it does illustrate a substrate underneath many ministry modes: that the *transfer of information* is the means of transformation. Within the church

6. Page, "Holographic Pastors."

we have the tendency to start a class, launch a program, or start a sermon series to master a spiritual topic. This perpetuates extraction, which has ramifications on what is left behind. The church has taken its cues from the halls of the academy or training seminars led by CEOs. This method has formed us toward specific ends. I doubt the New Testament church launched a weeknight program every time they wanted to learn something spiritual. We don't learn love in a classroom writing in notebooks with fill-in-the-blanks. When we're convinced we can, our heads detach from our bodies. We treat ourselves more like computers than organisms. We are not only energized by information but we crave it and seem to have a limitless appetite for it. The church worships the transaction of information and attendees love it. This delivery approach to learning in the church has had catastrophic effects on our rooted character of *practice* in the world.

All around us is this basic principle of addressing needs with information efficiently. The need to relieve pain is one example close to home. Physical pain is real and can be debilitating. The urgent issue becomes one of relieving the pain. In 1999 the Food and Drug Administration approved the drug Vioxx.[7] Vioxx was marketed by Merck and Company to treat osteoarthritis and acute pain conditions. And it did just that. Hundreds of thousands of people experienced the *efficient* relief of pain. Vioxx gained widespread acceptance among physicians treating patients with arthritis and other conditions. Worldwide, over 80 million people were prescribed Vioxx; yet the drug had long-term consequences that were not observed upon its initial release to the public. Between 88,000 and 140,000 cases of serious heart disease occurred from the effects of Vioxx. Blood clots, heart attacks, and further cardiovascular complications occurred. It is estimated that the drug caused 60,000 deaths and Merck's profit was upwards of 25 billion. Eventually, in 2004, Merck withdrew the drug from the market and paid out a measly $321 million in fines and lawsuits.[8] This moral has played out over and over. The most efficient way to address a challenge is not often the most vitally healthy way to address a challenge. This is the same with spiritual learning. Maybe you wonder why we should reform our ways of learning in the church because they appear to be working efficiently. On the surface they are "working," but at a significant liability to our practicing character.

7. Food and Drug Administration, "Vioxx and Drug Safety."
8. Herper, "Merck Withdraws Vioxx."

Within the ethos of the church the seeds for extracting information out of immersion may have began in the Sunday school movement, although I do not think that was ever the intention. The short-term effect of Sunday school was powerful but the long-term effect is what I'm evaluating. Sunday schools were originally schools for literacy learning. They were schools hosted inside churches to help poorer children learn how to read. The Industrial Revolution, spanning from the late 1700s to the early 1800s, sent many children into the work force all week long in factories.[9] Christian leaders sparked a concern for their growing handicap in reading and writing. Sunday became the day for children to get educated. Adults would attend the same classes alongside their children. The Sunday school movement grew and built large lecture halls, classrooms, and designated schools. Sunday school attendance was a near-universal aspect of childhood by the mid-nineteenth century. Slowly, as children were able to again attend school because of labor laws restricting children from working, children went back to learning how to read in public schools. Sunday school continued, morphing into religious education for adults and children. The Bible became the textbook. Sunday school gradually became the conduit for cognitive-driven discipleship; it centered on a building, a teacher, a curriculum, and an audience. Whether your church has Sunday school or not, this form of learning has been imported into many churches' modes of blueprinting spiritual transformation. *Is delivering information transformational?*

ASYMPTOMATIC INFORMATION CARRIERS

We accumulate spiritual information and are mesmerized by the accumulation. There is a literal emotional return in the dynamic of gobbling up information. The field of neuroscience has gathered some interesting research related to this information gold rush tendency. Two different brain imaging techniques have revealed that a specific area of the brain "lights up" when new information arrives, according to cognitive neuroscientists Mark Jung-Beeman and Edward Bowden of Northwestern University.[10] Our pleasure sensors feel a surge of satisfaction not unlike sexual arousal. We can become hooked on devouring information. "Addiction" may be a strong word but there is dependence created in the transfer of information. I can't tell

9. Wardle, *History of the Sunday School Movement*, 109–11.

10. Northwestern School of Medicine, "Cognitive Neuroscientists."

you how many times I've listened to a sermon, taken furious notes, walked away feeling utterly wowed by the communicator, and never assimilated what I heard into practice. I've been tempted to find a ripe time to opine on that information to someone else, as if I've integrated it into my own life. I sometimes feel the sermon podcast is one of the worst developments for the life of the church. Consuming sermons from a distant church, from a distant pastor who inevitably convinces us we're growing spiritually from this transaction, is an unfortunate turn in discipleship. What's more, we have a tendency to swear by the character of preachers we've never observed living out their sermons. The gap between information and immersion causes us to become ignorant to the consequences of discipleship. This is one of the ornery reasons my own church doesn't put our sermon podcast online for strangers. I'd prefer someone not think I am their pastor when I have never spent time with them. When our primary influences are from words rather than from warm bodies, *practice* will not take root. It's fully possible to have our opinions but not our practice changed. One thing I've learned is our stage personality is not the same as our seven-days-a-week personality. Often I think to myself: I can learn a lot from that person, but I would not follow that person. Brilliance does not always equal wisdom.[11] The modern church has become a colossal information Pez dispenser. We don't often see the need to evaluate our information delivery method because we believe the message is so good, so true. Our learning methods are generating legions of people stuffed to the gills with information but who are ironically not affected by the information they carry. In the world of viruses this is called an asymptomatic carrier. An asymptomatic carrier is one who carries an infectious disease but displays no symptoms and is unaffected by the disease themselves.[12] We have become asymptomatic information carriers unaffected by the content we gobble up. The very reason for this starts at the separation between *information* and *immersion*. We need to reform the whole way we see learning happening within the church. We must ask hard questions about who we are producing—consumers of information or practicing disciples?

God is subtle, but we're so conditioned to the loudest media. We love the wow of tightly presented pulpit messages. We love polished communicators from polished platforms. We love a punchy podcast. Yet when we inspect Jesus' teaching ministry he had serious frustration with the medium.

11. Fitch, @fitchest, Twitter.
12. Medical Dictionary, "Asymptomatic Carrier."

Jesus was very popular with crowds. Many people came because they wanted Jesus to cure them, and Jesus did. Then the crowds clamored for more, but often missed the message. Although he was popular, there often wasn't an intent to follow him in obedience. We have the same occurrence today in the miracle of our communication. We champion the spectacle of a captivating communicator but practice rarely flows from those consumptive forms. I'm not anti-preaching but I think it needs to be put in its place.

IMMERSED AND INTERTWINED

We intuitively know that our most essential transformative learning happens in *immersive* spaces with relational *intertwinement*. The vast majority of Christians are not learning through the beautiful collision of close-rub, life-on-life involvement in the scope of the neighborhood. Yet churches still pour most of their resources, most of their marketing, most of their inertia in the direction of structures that attract and extract. I get the pleasure of meandering around the country a little bit to coach church planters attempting to start new communities. I find it commonplace for a pastor/leader to barely have learned within the primary space of proximity and intimacy. As I poke and prod around this personal narrative, often what pops up is a level of sadness. Few know the delight and development of learning this way. It's a foreign world for most leaders so we build islands with our collection of information and commentaries. Maybe that's why we prop up the system. Many leaders have little to no orientation for learning outside one-way delivery vehicles.

When the majority of our spiritual formation takes place in the brick and mortar of a church building we build a habit of separation, whether that's our intention or not. As a kid I remember summers when school was out, getting up in the morning and scheming up my play plans for the day. My brother and I would watch some cartoons and inevitably my mom would say, "Okay boys it's time to go play outside, you're not staying in here all day." She was right. The adventures were outside, not sitting on a couch when it was eighty-five and sunny. We must begin to understand that separation happens naturally when so much of our spiritual work happens in our own designated sanctified spaces. We've easily constructed little compounds that separate us, educate us, instruct us, and even offer us therapeutic experiences, but the extraction progressively removes us from the tilling and toiling within community and neighborhood relationships.

I've been a pastor for a little more than fifteen years and have contributed to extraction. In the past I've communicated that all the action is at one of our many church events and programs. "Sign up, join up, show up, get filled up." Are we conditioning people that God is in here and not out there? We move from from one sermon to the next, one project to the next, one program launch to the next, just praying and hoping our information is hitting pay dirt. Michael Frost states, "Worshiping God does not mean bringing those religious things (over there) into our life (over here)."[13] We need to break the hypnosis we experience by extracting truth-based information. Gradually the church has built a compound of learning rather than relational laboratories for conversing, listening, reflecting, and practicing. We will lay out a new pathway forward in our chapter on "Practicing Community."

When we explore Jesus' method for discipleship it becomes clear how information that rolled off the tongue of the Messiah was always immersed in an embodied situation. Jesus spoke often of the invitational nature of the kingdom of God. He taught about the nature of God's love for all, especially for perceived outsiders. We come upon a passage that reads like this in Luke 9:11–13: "People who are well don't need a doctor! It's those who are wounded who do! Now go away and learn the meaning of this, 'It isn't your sacrifices and your worship I want—I want you to be merciful.' For I have come to invite the hurting, not the self-righteous, back to God." The sting of this information is small and scant when read extracted from immersion. We can simply cut and paste this verse into a sermon or a spiritual program and hope the Holy Spirit does its thing, but that would be a shame. Now imagine you're a first-century disciple and Jesus drags you into "table fellowship" with notorious sinners. Jesus has you feasting, reclining, and conversing with people that could ruin your reputation. As disciples walk with the Messiah they look around and find themselves at a raucous party. Jesus immerses you in a practice of showing mercy, closing the gap between so-called sinner and saint. Maybe your skin crawls; maybe you're filled with anxiety, questions, and even some disorientation. What is this about? What is the rabbi showing us, teaching us? Yet you are learning just by being in it with Jesus. Then some religious inspectors pop in on your party and ask a zinger of a question: "Why does your teacher eat with tax collectors and sinners?" Maybe you don't even know how to answer. You reach into your mind for some brilliant response but you don't have one. You are caught off guard. Yet you are immersed, maybe even plunged

13. Frost, *Incarnate*, 98–99.

into the information that Jesus will offer. "People who are well don't need a doctor! It's those who are wounded who do! Now go away and learn the meaning of this . . . ." You are being exposed to a discipleship course that moves you deeper into the world rather than higher up in the synagogue. Jesus' *method* became his message. Defined by the Messiah, to learn is to participate in an interactive relationship *with* others. There is integrity in this learning approach. Jesus didn't preach about "serving the oppressed," he served the oppressed, taught about it as he did it, and invited disciples to immerse themselves their minds and bodies in it. Jesus hung out with the poor and immersed the disciples. Jesus ate and drank in community and immersed the disciples. Jesus explained the kingdom to others and immersed the disciples. This immersion was not haphazard or accidental. Discipleship is not a "fundamentalist thing," it's the only way to close the gap between our minds and our bodies.

We have too much dependency on information-based, content-delivery teaching. We have deconstruction to do on the ways we learn together. The rooted character of practice has been the victim of our apparently productive learning modes. We must experiment with refreshed, vintage ways and then carve a path forward. Recovering embodied learning goes far beyond hip new strategies. The rabbinic learning form Jesus modeled has much to teach us (to be explored in a later chapter). There may have been a time when closer-knit practice with others occurred more organically, but we currently live in a fragmented, information-consuming society that will require an intentional disruption of our slide towards spiritual hypocrisy.[14] We know deep in our bones that we must restore the severed connections between *information* and *immersion*. The future of the church must seek rooted ways of learning that restore relational practice. This is the subterranean church.

14. Scandrette, *Practicing the Way of Jesus*, 45–46.

4

Expedited Production

I USED TO BE in a band, and a pretty good one, I might say. I loved the creative sphere of songwriting, the recording process, and the merging of multiple musicians. In our heyday, when I was 20 pounds thinner with full head of glorious hair, we played on some pretty big stages, won a couple of competitions, opened up for some headliners, and got a little airplay. I remember when we recorded and produced our first single. The feeling of a finished product was electrifying after a month of sweaty work in a studio. The medium of distribution was the infamous MySpace. I remember the surge of anticipation as we uploaded our single onto our customized MySpace page. I was glued to that web page for almost a month. I actually got sick of hearing my own song, but I was mesmerized by the ticker counting up how many hits our single was getting, watching it go from 0 listens to 5 to 100 to 1000. I plastered myself to that computer to see how fast our music would make an impact. The speed at which I could measure our impact as a band had emotional control over me. I desire things expedited, to move faster, to offer me a quick sense of gratification. Much of this undulation in me is related to how I've framed *impact* in the past. When we think of impact it is often infused with an expedited fruition of our goals.

IDOLATRY OF IMPACT

I'm drawn in by passionate people, passionate purposes, and passionate public displays. As a bit of an activist, what stirs me up is ardent change of the status quo. *Do you resonate with this desire?* I've traveled to refugee camps in Kenya, the streets in Philadelphia, villages in Guyana, and the boroughs of New York City, brimming with idealism, following through on my convictions. I want to see what is wrong made right, what is broken healed up; this is a thunderous impulse within me. On the Richter scale of my life it is events that exemplified sudden disruptive change that seem to gain my attention: the lone man standing in front of tanks in Tiananmen Square or Martin Luther nailing the Ninety-Five Theses to the Wittenberg door or Rosa Parks refusing to give up her seat on the bus. These stories have become our template for catalyzing change in the modern era. In their differing ways they all made an impact. These are our heroes and rightly so. We love our heroes. Heroes have great capabilities to make things happen. We admire their ability to shape destiny according to their powerful actions. This becomes our mental framework for creating impact. The unintended consequence of the exaltation of these heroes is that these images of impact hold a mythological power over us.[1] The picture of change in our public consciousness is decisive, expeditious, and makes headlines. We don't really have a category or an emotional tolerance for incremental, quiet, careful, patient impact. In the American consciousness we might actually label that ineffective, indifferent, and potentially lazy. Any level of restraint appears counterproductive to movement. The avatar of patience does not typically go viral. The church has a thing for speed as does the larger culture, but often we baptize "fast" in Christian lingo. So much of our language reflects this *idolatry of impact.* This impact doctrine—"let's change culture," "let's change the world," "let's start a movement," "let's do something great"—makes quiet faithful presence in our cities seem like it's for the birds when it's probably the most courageous way to live.

Just recently a well-known Christian pastor/author was caught fudging the rankings on the *New York Times* best-seller list with the mass purchasing his own of books. The intent was to inflate sales quickly. The church's statement from their publicist exposes the undercurrent of expedited impact. "We will explore any opportunity that helps us to get the message out, while striving to remain above reproach in the process. Whether we're talking about technology, music, marketing, or whatever, we want greater impact for the name of Jesus as rapidly as possible. That's what we're all about and have been since 1996."[2] This statement is not an obscure sentiment.

1. Carlyle, *Heroes*, 88–91.
2. Smith, "Unreal Sales for Mark Driscoll."

"Impact as rapidly as possible" is a tidal wave drowning out our character. The mad grab for impact while giving cursory lip service to "God's glory" has become normal. We should be very cautious about wrapping "impact" in biblicism knowing that within us resides a ravenous desire for emotional return and rave reviews. Resisting our slavish need to press the accelerator seems counterintuitive when so much needs to be accomplished. We are narrowly focused on attendance and property expansion because of the idolatry of impact. American brands of Christianity have crazy eyes and a ferocious appetite for impact and especially for it expedited. We have an addiction to the substance that impact offers us, a quantifiable sensation that something significant is happening. We worship data that measures our impact, our scope, our size, and our propagating power. We have blurred the lines between character and information; there is no greater shame than having an organization that is not charting upward at a steady clip. This pressure, this idolatry of impact, has penetrated and poisoned our explanations for how God moves. We encase our own leadership desires for instant significance in the language of faith.

No one is more vilified than Judas because of his betrayal of Christ. John 12:4–6 describes Judas's actions, saying that he chose to betray Christ, he wasn't forced into it. Christ gave him the opportunity to change his mind, but Judas allowed Satan access to his heart. Do we really understand, however, why he did what he did? Was he utterly vile and reprehensible? Was he "special" and thus not really responsible for his actions? In answering these questions we must get to know Judas better to understand what motivated him, to understand what drew him towards his actions. First, we note that there are similarities between Judas and the others. Like them all, he was looking for the Messiah and thought Christ might be the one. Like them all, he was willing to follow regardless of the "hardships." Like them all, he assumed that Christ would launch an earthly kingdom. It is necessary to note that he was not markedly different from the other twelve disciples. He was their treasurer so he was trusted by the apostles, receiving the job over Matthew who had worked with money all his life. Each apostle started from a point of weakness as Jesus was discipling them toward transformation. Judas seems to have been a man who liked things controlled and predictable. He objected to Mary's sacrifice, seeing it as wasteful. Jesus was a man Judas could not control. Jesus' plans were not efficient, not predicable, not guaranteeing certain outcomes. When Jesus started talking about death, which would be perceived as failure, rather than rebellion that would be perceived as action, Judas became anxious. He wanted the impact of the kingdom now. He wanted Israel free from Rome now. Judas wanted the prestige, the power, the positional influence now. Jesus' teaching about "the first being last" and "I came to serve" could be perceived as a hindrance to movement in achieving these goals. Judas wanted a leader who would catalyze an organization. Judas had disdain for the snail's pace at which the Messiah stirred up change against the oppressive empire. By the time Jesus and his disciples arrived in Jerusalem to celebrate the Passover, Judas had grown impatient with the lack of progress. As a last, desperate move Judas chose to hit the nitro button, seeking to speed things up in order to force the situation. Judas was a go-getter, a pragmatist seeking radical return on investment. We all have Judas-junk inside us. We can easily scapegoat Judas because of his betrayal but it's his unchecked, unexposed, unrestrained ambitions that fueled his actions. Our good intentions, our desires for kingdom impact easily get mixed into the petri dish of our church ambitions. A church with the faithful qualities of fruits of the Spirit simply does not go viral, and I'm not sure these virtues lead to rapid expansion. We don't learn how to make a church from personalities like Steve Jobs, Jimmy Fallon, or Donald Trump. Fortune 500 companies and captivating entertainers build lucrative kingdoms but not the kingdom of God. The church that our future needs is one with real roots, whether they are those of a bonsai or an oak. We must start there.

What lurks beneath in our ministry leadership?

Do our church systems perpetuate and reward this private ambition for impact?

FRIGHTENED OF ORDINARINESS

Impact has connotations of a meteor slamming into a region, leaving behind a massive hole. Our powerful portraits of making an impact have done just that, left us with gaping holes, craters in the formation of community and in our presence in places. There is a dynamic to impact that disguises these catastrophic holes. At points in my life I've not recognized them. The sheer force of doing something that *matters for God* puts a ringing in your ears that numbs your senses to the way you dwell in the world. We're fairly good at making an impact but deficient at the particularities of patience that makes space for incarnation. Leaders who are frightened of *ordinariness* create church cultures that overreach for measurable impact that gives their ministry or project perceived legitimacy. The race to make an impact and tally our victories has infiltrated our character. Leaders who crave results build churches that crave results. Christians who have too much of their identity wrapped up in production tend to be highly competitive and defensive. We long to be extraordinary rather than ordinary. So we attempt to find a way to matter and to matter quickly. This creates disequilibrium at our core, making us anxious to be exquisite in our respective spheres. We have deep discontentment with circumstances that are not "blowing up" or "taking off." I can feel the tremor in my soul, causing irritation in my attitude as I wait for my wife to pick up lunch for me. There is a voice in my head saying "why is it taking so long?" The particle of this feeling rises up in my throat and forms my inner demands. I become acutely aware of what I want, when I want it, and how I want to feel when I get it. There is a codependent interplay between the urgency in a leader's heart and the character of "impact" a church will develop. Our churches are in an all-out sprint to gain vivacious traction through the next sermon series, worship event, or church plant. The church has embraced a microwave mentality, believing we can nuke everything—disciples, justice, growth, evangelism, revival, and salvations. Eugene Peterson has said, "There is a great market for religious experience in our world; there is little enthusiasm for cultivating the virtue of patience."[3] We've accepted the measuring tools of velocity as a way to interpret if God is doing something, if God's Spirit is moving. This is not a kingdom-of-God metric; it is an American cultural metric. We idolize impact. The Bible says little about the skills necessary to produce exponential results. Rather, it heralds character every time.[4] We prioritize immediate results rather than prioritizing patience. Our demand for impact has done violence to our rootedness. We need to take a machete to this overgrown ideology of impact.

3. Peterson, *A Long Obedience*, 88–89.
4. Challies, "Character is King."

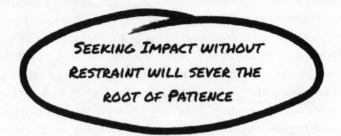

SEEKING IMPACT WITHOUT
RESTRAINT WILL SEVER THE
ROOT OF PATIENCE

MOLASSES MOVEMENT

In biblical history, the intertestamental period was a long season of time between the voice of the prophet Malachi in 420 BC (closing the Old Testament period) and the first-century-AD voice of John the Baptist (opening the New Testament period). This is roughly a 400-year period.[5] This is a span where God said next to nothing to the people of God; God was silent. In this long cold winter, the dear Jewish people sat under Persian empirical rule and eventually the conquest of Alexander the Great, which ushered in the Hellenistic period. Jews under Grecian domination were imperialized with the Greek language and ideas throughout the ancient world. The Greek culture sought to eliminate the unique identity of the Hebrew people. There was no resisting the dominance of Greek culture. So powerful was this Hellenization that even after Rome conquered the Jews, the Greek culture continued within the Roman Empire. Please put yourself in the skin of a people waiting. Step into the shoes of people stuck crying out for deliverance. God seemed slow. He moved at a molasses pace from the perspective of anyone on the ground.

Are we okay with God moving slowly?

Jesus himself was being baited to succumb to expediting impact. During his temptation in the wilderness in Luke 4, Satan terrorized Jesus with sarcastic questions targeting the immediacy of his significance in the world. The enemy poked a stick at his humanity. He quipped, "If you are the Son of God . . . ," as if to say "if you are all that . . . why don't people know by now?" Jesus had been lingering around the Nazareth neighborhood for three decades and nobody had a clue who he was. *Is this acceptable?* How can God in Jesus accept these slow terms for impact? The enemy was poking at that

5. Surburg, *Introduction to the Intertestamental Period*, 31–32.

internal clock ticking on our perceived chance to prove how prolific we are or how prolific our ministry is. Jesus practiced restraint.

Does our image of impact have any space for 400 years of silence?

Does God have to move fast for God to be moving?

Rooted patience can be found in people like Simeon. "At this time a man named Simeon was living in Jerusalem. Simeon was a good man. He loved God and was waiting for God to save the people of Israel" (Luke 2:22). And Anna. "She was the daughter of Phanuel from the tribe of Asher, and she was very old. And now she was eighty-four years old. Night and day she served God in the temple by praying and often going without eating" (Luke 2:36–37). We need leaders with the rooted character of patience but more so we need churches with the character of patience.

There are many other snapshots in the Scriptures of how sloooow God moves. Even now as you read the word *slow* it might seem like a slam on God. Slow has picked up all kinds of baggage. We plunk slow into the bucket labeled bad. We see it as a negative thing to *go slow*. Might I suggest we've picked up this connotation not from God's character but from the character of our culture? Jesus compared his kingdom to a mustard seed— almost invisible, unimpressive to the eye. Yet he assures us it will grow into something magnificent that will cover the whole earth (Matt 13:31–32). This smallness was a scandal then and it is a scandal today. In our efforts to mimic the ancient great cities of Rome, Athens, and Corinth, and our desire for "real disciples" who aren't like Thomas and Judas, we end up chasing after goals that aren't God's.[6] The way we push and program for impact has cultivated impatience rather than the mature character of restraint. The future of the church must embrace slow not as masochism but as a missional character. As the church father Tertullian said, "Impatience is, as it were, the original sin in the eyes of the Lord. For, to put it in a nutshell, every sin is to be traced back to impatience. I find the origin of impatience in the Devil himself."[7] It is God's nature to be patient.

6. Scazzero, *The Emotionally Healthy Church*, 111–12.

7. Tertullian, *Of Patience*.

MICROWAVE MENTALITY

In the book *In Praise of Slowness* author Carl Honore exposes the cult of speed. He uses the phase "the Age of Rage" to expound upon the chronic hurry we feel and have allowed to drive us forward.[8] "Have I gone completely insane? . . . my whole life has turned into an exercise in hurry, in packing more and more into every hour. I'm a Scrooge with a stopwatch, obsessed with saving every last scrap of time." Larry Dossey, an American physician, calls this "time-sickness."[9] Time-sickness is an obsession with how long things take to materialize. Speed has been knighted as king in our subconscious. A Jewish rabbi once told me that "wisdom is simply slowing down long enough to see." Wisdom is not special intelligence for an informed few. Rather wisdom slows down long enough to ponder the ramifications of our choices on other humans. Turbo-church speaks in vernacular of how quickly God moves and how quickly he changes lives. We all have the tendency to let our talk outpace our practice. We must discipline the viral chatter we participate in, tempering our adolescent exuberance when speaking about how dynamic we think we are. Communicating *impact* is immediate, seems direct and uncomplicated, and creates instantaneous response to stimulate energy. Our grand language should lag way, way behind our action. American life can feel like an insane asylum pulsating with noise, technology, information, and competition. The church does not need to add to that buzz. The acceleration of culture is clear but the church should be introducing contours of resistance to this force. We need permission to slow down.

The Tyranny of Demand

In Michael Moss's book *Salt Sugar Fat,* he speaks of the demand for speed. "Convenience is the great additive which must be designed, built in, combined, blended, interwoven, injected, inserted, or otherwise added to or incorporated in products or services if they are to satisfy today's demanding public. The controlling denominator of the consumer mind-set is demand."[10] This modern value of "demand" trains us to see slowness as "wasted time." We're not accomplishing anything! We can do this more

8. Honore, *In Praise of Slowness,* 33–34.

9. Dossey, *Space, Time and Medicine,* 22–23.

10. Moss, *Salt Sugar Fat,* 21.

efficiently! In Michael Pollan's 2001 book *The Botany of Desire*, he explores the nature of humanity's growing desire for immediacy in food, which is reflected in the way we selectively grow, breed, and genetically engineer our potatoes. There is a demand for French fries that is forcing suppliers to speed up the growth of potatoes to unnatural rates. Demand within our culture compels us to compromise our ethics.[11] In the same way, we live in a frenetic digital age that mistakes information for wisdom and makes patience a liability for capitalizing on opportunities.

How does the church respond to demand?

Within the church, demand should cause us to slow things down, frustrate consumer demand, and push us into the space of discretion. Speed is violent on human relations and should provoke the call of local church communities to be islands of patience in a world of speed.[12] There is a consumer doctrine that prescribes convenience and customizability for optimum product satisfaction. There was very little that was convenient or optimum about life together in the first-century church. We don't pursue patience for altruistic grandeur. Patience makes space for people as organisms, not machines, and makes space for God as mysterious, not predictable. Whenever we pitch patience in the way we practice being the church we are tempted to manufacture the appearance of change. Patience is a mind-set but it is also a guardrail for protecting the human spirit from corruption.

In my own church plant I've been tempted to bail on slowness. I've been tempted to microwave it! I've always had a holy love for Christian community: an enfleshed common life as a witness to the lordship of Christ. Here's the thing: the cultivation of community is head-poundingly slow. At one point in the cultivation of our faith community I felt we were not growing fast enough. We needed more energy and more people energetic about what we were doing. So we launched a spectacular worship gathering with a sweet hipster band, candles and liturgical prayers, and my electric sermons. This is the formula for microwaving a movement. We quadrupled in size, growing quickly, but something wasn't right. Comment after comment revolved around the quality of our worship and the pithy, insightful, story-filled way I preached. I remember driving home one night with my wife. I should have been on a numbers high but I wasn't. I could only think about the stress of

11. Pollan, *The Botany of Desire*, 73–74.

12. Virillo, *Speed & Politics*, 36–37.

discipling this many people in an expedited way. Thankfully, with confident grace in her eyes, my wife said, "This is not us. This does not feel right, it's too fast, not patient enough." I love it when my wife drops unassuming truth bombs like that. She was right. The virtue of patience had to give us a little swat on the tush. People are easily turned into pieces to manage and the channels of relationship do not have time to be nurtured, treasured, and prioritized. The body of Christ can easily lose its *body* and merely become an *audience*. This template for church in the West takes relationships and converts them into transactions, forming a market. We become subjects of this market, caught in a producer-consumer delivery system.

Patience is often seen as a quaint attribute to apply when waiting for something good to happen—waiting for that perfect job, or for the real estate agent to call us back with a "yes." Yet in the narrative of Scripture, patience is not quaint—it is a character trait forged in the grueling, unpredictable marathon of joining God's messy mission in the world.[13] When you think "mission" don't think army occupations or corporate sales goals that drive us to string up the "Mission Accomplished" banner so we can celebrate our achievements. Mission in God's kingdom is neither linear nor tally-able in this fashion. God is not positioned outside the world, seeking to dominate—rather, God is situated in the world, striving with us, hurting with us, working from within the chaos we inhabit, seeking to mature us and move us forward. God has designed a world that functions more like a temperamental garden than an interlocking engine. God works with the existing material of human choices, human freedom, and the human will to cultivate something glorious. There is breathing room and real possibility within God's dreams for the kingdom to flourish. Jesus is King and his desires *will* be done on earth as it is in heaven, but this does not mean his will is meticulous or unmalleable.[14] God is ruler but his status does not extinguish our free status. This is why patience is a core attribute of God. God does not control people, refusing to override our capacity to volunteer or resist. Patience is required when you're working *with* people, not commandeering them. God is patient with human collaboration and we see this in the way Jesus invites, intrigues, entices, and challenges—but never forces. God must have patience to coexist and partner with humanity and so should we. The Scriptures call God's people to learn trust, to learn

13. McKnight, *A Long Faithfulness*, 33.
14. Boyd, *God at War*, 44.

mystery, to learn wonder and learn restraint when we want to shove things over the precipice to get them going.

SUPERSEDING OUR LIMITS

To be human is to be subjected to time, space, and resources; yet we disdain our predicament. To acknowledge our weakness is considered a weakness itself in the West. To confess you are not articulate, a slow learner, not witty, not magnetic, or unable to grasp concepts is fatal to a reputation. We are conditioned to overpower our inadequacies and deny the boundaries of time. Jesus models for us a bumping up against these constraints. "Jesus left and returned to his hometown with his disciples. The next Sabbath he taught and many of the people who heard him were amazed and asked, 'How can he do all this? Where did he get such power to work these miracles? Isn't he the carpenter the son of Mary? Aren't James, Joseph, Judas, and Simon his brothers? Don't his sisters still live here in our town?' But Jesus could not work any miracles there. He was surprised that the people did not have any faith" (Mark 6:1–6). God in Christ submits himself to limits; this is humbling and I'm sure frustrating, to have the *ability* to do something but not do it. Jesus embraced the limits offered to him by the Father. God in Christ subjected himself to a mom and dad, had to learn to sit up, to walk, to go potty, to bathe, to learn all the things humans do. Jesus didn't fall out of heaven fully formed. The fullness of the Godhead dwelled in Jesus and he was relegated to doing household chores for an allowance. The all-powerful God knows something about embracing limits for the purpose of mission. Jesus knows the nakedness of being seen, of being slowed. How can we think that the way of mission is any different for us than it was for the incarnation of God in Christ?

Superseding our limits of time, money, age, and location tempts us into a silly form of omnipotence. There is a myth floating around that we can "do it all." In the movie *Limitless* an aspiring writer named Eddie, played by Bradley Cooper, is feeling like a loser after being dumped by his girlfriend and making no progress in his career as an author. Eddie connects with his former brother-in-law Vernon, who gives him an experimental drug that increases brain capacity and will help him write his book at lightning speed. Eddie uses the drug and the results are impressive. He takes more pills, gets a haircut, new clothes, and finishes the book in four days. He learns piano and a few new languages within hours. Eddie becomes addicted to the prestige and power that his new mind affords him but it begins to demolish his character from the inside out. Certainly this is an exaggerated picture of superseding limits but images of that narrative do tempt us. Self-imposed limits for the sake of incarnation seem like a ridiculous notion, yet this is exactly what the future of the church must discern.

Our urgency to make an impact can pull us away from patience required to dwell *with* people. The faster we move towards our goals the more we see relating as a hindrance. The most meaningful impact is the space where the human spirit touches another human spirit. This is what God modeled for us in his humanity. Nothing can replace the power of the kingdom of God in proximity, in staying long enough to make eye contact, to touch with faithful presence. As one who's spent a lot of time in hospitals I've observed this "touch" wired into our human fiber. Most neonatal intensive care units are full of buttons, little flashing lights, and the steady hum of technology. The machines that line the rooms are safeguarding the most fragile human lives. Babies in the neonatal intensive care unit are clinging to life, but sometimes parents and nurses can't be there to offer reassurance. That's why many hospitals have volunteer "cuddlers" come in.[15] There is a science around human touch and the need for nearness is not exclusive to babies. Ever wonder why a hug at the end of a long, grueling day feels so great? We're hardwired to seek out physical touch. When we get that touch our brains reward us by releasing a hormone/neurotransmitter called oxytocin. This oxytocin is also known as the "cuddle" hormone. It's in our human genome to experience this type of proximity. Is it any wonder that four times the Apostle Paul instructs the church at Rome, at Corinth, and at Thessalonica to greet each other with a kiss? There is something sacramental about proximity, the closeness, the accessibility in which the people of God are to gather. Certainly leaders have abused touch but we should not let devils steal our virtue of touchability.

As we contemplate God's movement towards our world we see Jesus came with more than rhetoric to turn things upside down. He invited disciples to immerse in real time as their means of unlearning and relearning. We see that God in Jesus also shook off selfish ambition in order to open up space for a deep, abiding presence with people. Finally we see God is in no rush and the urgency to make an impact is turned on its head as Jesus exercises patience with the human will. We need to reorganize our churches with these characters embedded in our identity.

15. Wright and Netter, "Power of Human Touch."

PART TWO

The Future of the Rooted Church

5

Submerging into the World

RADICAL WORLD

I WALKED INTO A bookstore the other day to waste some time before an appointment. Bookstores are having a tough go these days but I still like the touch and smell of paper and ink. Coffee in hand, I wandered over to the religion section to pick through the literary clutter. I did a little perusing but gradually my mind was putting together a pattern: there were a slew of books with the word *radical* on the cover. Really, it took me aback. *Radical Possibilities, Radical Womanhood, Radical Hospitality, Radical Love, Radical Reformission*—and this does not include the books with *radical* in the subtitle. I'm not sure I've ever noticed it before. Radical is a "thing," a big thing: add the word *radical* to whatever your deal is and it acquires maximum impact. It's true, try it: radical lawn care, radical vacuuming, radical sandwich making, radical coffee drinking (of which I'd be a fan). Honestly, I'd prefer something radicalized over something non-radicalized. Why is that? I want to explore what it means to be *rooted* in relation to being *radical*.

Being radical has taken on a life of its own in the Christian subculture. The overall sentiment for combining radical and the church has been around in Christianity for a while, as reflected in sayings like "on fire" or "sold out." Stadiums are packed every year with eager Christians recharging their emotional batteries to become planet shakers. I've traveled the circuit of Christian conferences over the years and incessantly heard the indirect verbiage of fear. Being radical has leveraged so much traction off of our fears of being lukewarm; yet the rhetoric used to oppose lukewarm living rarely actualizes close to the ground in proximity to localized people. Radical is frequently described as a journey up the mountain, where we leave our attachments and worldliness and slowly make our way to the peak. Our fears of wasting our lives often sling us upward in a nervous hunt for maximizing our faith. Fear seldom sends forth rhythms of love (1 Jn 4:18). Our current frameworks for being "radical" squirm with incredibly individualistic fanfare, firing us out to make some noise but making us incapable of dwelling in a place. This anxiety to outrun the unsettling horror that "I just might be ordinary" usually stirs up random radical activity but eventually fizzles out. I'm convinced *radical* is more than a pithy word we use to add a little extra oomph. It's more than a word; it's a symbol, a way we survey ourselves. We aspire to be radical as followers of Jesus, but I suspect there is an upward trajectory to our notions that is covertly ruinous. Our current notions of *radical* need a serious renovation.

ESCALATOR INTO THE HEAVENS

Humans have an appetite for altitude. Whether it be on cocaine or the Apollo missions, what is it about the human condition that longs to lift away from earth?[1] One part of the answer is this: from positions of height we get a detached perspective. The chaos of streets fall into some kind of order. The patterns of our lives and the maze of choices suddenly become clear to us. We are suckers for any claim that promises us revelation over and above our circumstances. We long to elevate. We reach for any technology that ushers a high into the nucleus accumbens area of our brains. We have utopian longings that something, somewhere will get us high enough that all things will become coherent. This clawing for a heightened experience shows up in the practices of hippies, mystics, and the modern Evangelical church. It was also the great hope of the space race. Part of the hope of going to the moon was that when people looked back on earth they would see how senseless war was and all humankind would be reconciled. Armstrong and Aldrin could see a lot when they stepped out onto the surface, but they couldn't see the atrocities continuing in Vietnam far below. To be radical is not to go farther and higher; it is not to become further detached from the

1. Brewin, "The Universe is Not Rigged."

messy minutiae of the world. To be radical is not to outrun the ordinariness of our existence.

Babel is the apex of humankind's ambition to go higher.[2] At the Tower of Babel we're given an angle on human civilization's drive to go upward with its own significance.[3] "Now the whole world had one language and a common speech. As people moved eastward, they found a plain in Shinar and settled there. They said to each other, 'Come, let's make bricks and bake them thoroughly.' They used brick instead of stone, and tar for mortar. Then they said, 'Come, let us build ourselves a city, with a tower that reaches to the heavens, so that we may make a name for ourselves . . .'" (Gen 11:1–4). There's an escalator enticing human potential to move away from the grime and grease of human groundedness. We have God-given abilities that, combined with human ambitions, naturally lead to an upward orbit. So much of our popular imagination around being "radical" is padded with skyward, risk-taking language that is knotted together with how we view God in our mind's eye. When most imagine God they filter out anything that is not superhuman, supersized, powerful, and larger than life. Just forming the word *God* with our lips conjures up a Zeus-like character who is sitting on a golden throne high above the earth.[4] The Israelites, who had barrels of content in the Old Testament, interpreted that God would present himself in a way that would elevate them. Yet God in Christ rebels against this tidal wave of elevation. Jesus' victory wouldn't be miraculously blasted to millions as undeniable proof of his legitimacy. Jesus did not appear Godlike from a human perspective when he was dying on a wooden cross. The Apostle Paul spoke of the cross as the weakness and foolishness of God (1 Cor 1:18). As a historical person, Jesus was not as magnificent as the gods of the Pantheon.[5] The way in which God wielded his glory did not look so glorious in comparison. Jesus' own disciples were as confused about glory as we are today. At one point when they're arguing about glory, Jesus overhears their pontificating and states emphatically "you don't know what you are talking about." Jesus knows that glory essentially is to *reveal* one's true character. Jesus follows up by expounding on glory and in his subversive way unfolds what God's character is really like: "I have not come to be served but to serve and to lay my life down." This is God's glory. We

2. Holscaw, "The Fall as False Unity."

3. Ibid.

4. Frank, *A Gentler God,* 134–35.

5. Caputo, *The Weakness of God,* 90–92.

are trying to blaze up an escalator but God is on his way down. Jesus' arrival to planet earth is a definitive exclamation of God's framework for ministry. God wears skin, is made flesh and blends into a neighborhood. God was fashioning a bond with his created project, establishing foundations, cultivating roots, going subterranean. Christ was learning how to be human as the baseline for his mission; eating and drinking with fringe friends, laughing with them, playing with them, and working alongside them. Jesus is our prototype for being in the world; he is our crucial clarification on being radical.[6]

MADE FOR THIS PLACE

I recently saw a bumper sticker that said "I am not of this world." This statement is symbolic of a strong sentiment rampant in Christian culture: "We don't really want to be present here." But what the future of the church desperately needs is a thicker presence. In my favorite Pixar movie, *Wall-E*, a colony of people retreat to a spaceship that keeps them separated from the pollution, dirt, and mess in the world. A cute little robot does their dirty work on the earth while they float in luxury among the stars. They design a customized experience that meets all their needs in their spaceship. We get a glimpse of life on the spaceship with its sparkly cleanness and readily available services, but it's had a dehumanizing effect. People are more selfish, narcissistic, petty, self-indulgent, and individualistic. Somehow, being removed from the blight on earth has cut off their roots and strangled the virtue of their humanness. Not only does the world need their presence, but they need the world in return. This reminds me of a modern worship song I heard once, that repeated the refrain "this world has nothing for me." I understand the idea, but it's unhelpful for our imaginations. We need the world: it challenges us to love and look into the face of others. When we cushion ourselves from the world we make enemies of the world. God uses the world as our school to take know-it-all students and humble their stiff stubbornness to incarnation. Rootedness can expose our hearts' own unfitness. It reminds me a bit of how a trainer at the local gym told me that working out was going to make me feel soreness in muscles I forgot I had. She had suggested I do a round of squats, so I did. Afterward I could barely walk for three days and she called it a "good hurt." This is the nature of cultivating roots. There are muscles of love that are irritated when they are

6. Wright, *How God Became King*, 112–13.

introduced to incarnation. The church cannot perpetuate the abstraction of "being incarnational." It's time we reorient around incarnational non-negotiables. To proclaim the glory of the incarnate God we must live into the *good hurt* of incarnation. Proclamation of the kingdom of God does not happen through bumper stickers, celebrity pulpits, T-shirts, bands, politicians, legislation, Twitter feeds, or sports stars that mention God's name on TV. The world's ears are bleeding from the onslaught of better marketing, sharper words, and clever spins on our message. We need a radicalism uninterested in making a statement and taking a public stand. We need less spiritual bombast and more rooted love in the world. The resurrection work of Christ first must pass through the corridor of incarnation. Nothing, nothing, nothing replaces the spiritual, biblical, and anthropological phenomenon of up-close proximity and presence. When we organize our churches in ways that incarnation is left scrambling to keep up with, we demoralize the planting of a kingdom tree. Incarnation calls us into a subterranean way of ministering to the world.

GOING UNDERGROUND

The Quakers of the eighteenth century were very aware that in their own past they had slaves. It was not enough to clear their conscience by confessing their sins; they had to move from confession to a solidarity that would cost them. Living under a government that believed people could be property didn't call them to contend for legislation—rather, it called them to drench their convictions in incarnation. The Quakers participated in one of the most revolutionary, quiet, insurrectionary, and subterranean movements in America history. The Underground Railroad, a spider web network of people, guided fugitive slaves from the South to the North and to Canada.[7] It was not led by any single organization or person. Rather, it was a submerged network fueled by convictions. The escape network was not literally underground or a railroad. It was figuratively "underground" in the sense of being a rebellion that remained off the radar. The Underground Railroad consisted of meeting points, secret routes, transportation, safe houses, and assistance provided by abolitionist sympathizers. Quakers generally organized in small clusters, maintaining secrecy. For the slave, running away was anything but easy. Escaping the slaveholder was the first challenge. Often times an outsider would pose as a slave, join a plantation,

7. Siebert, *The Underground Railroad*, 56–57.

and then guide the runaways northward. The fugitives would travel during the night. By foot they would move many miles to the next home, where they would hide, rest, and eat. Without a visible and institutional structure the Underground Railroad effectively moved thousands of slaves northward each year—according to one estimate moving 100,000 slaves between 1810 and 1850.[8] Committees consisting of a few families sprang up in cities throughout New York, Philadelphia, and Boston. These committees gathered resources to provide food, lodging, and money to help former slaves settle into new communities. Quakers harboring escaped slaves had their homes visited and searched. A relative of mine bought an early 1800s home years ago in hopes of renovating it. During the renovation they discovered a hidden compartment between two walls that was large enough to hide a person. They did some research and found their house was part of the Underground Railroad. It's unbelievable to think a frightened, hungry, exhausted human hid out in your living room walls. It's even more unbelievable to think hundreds of people kept these prolific, ongoing actions under wraps, concealed from the popular eye. A deep, substantial, spiritual movement labored forward without the channels of publicity, celebrity, and institutionalism. A chain of human incarnation was the generator and sustainer. Lives were rescued, countercultural ethics were held tightly, and change was wrought. The spirit of The Underground Railroad *embodied* is a spirit I hope we can learn from. This was in some respects subterranean. We need ingenuity and imagination for what happens below the ground, beyond the landscaping that most churches fixate on.

Do we have hope for a vital church that goes off the grid?

Do we have vision for a church that refuses to lean on excessiveness, expediting, and extracting?

VINTAGE VIRTUES FOR THE FUTURE

Western Christianity is in a pinch. Things are not as they once were. There is a titanic shift occurring under our feet, and we can certainly feel it. This has ushered in disequilibrium. Some are reaching for their weapons and others are fortifying their shelters. It's easy to be disconcerted. We are straddling two worlds—the history of the church in the West and the future

8. Ibid, 58.

of the church in the West. It is an uncomfortable space that pushes us up against the wall, demanding an answer for how we'll progress. Yet the future vitality of the church is not in wielding the tools of relevancy, ingenuity, and efficiency. These tools have potentially led us to be excessive, expedited, and extracted. Evangelicalism is destined to die of its own success . . . constantly under the burden of reinventing the wheel and fading into exhaustion.[9] Rather, we need to lean in and listen to the reverberation of an earlier Christianity. We must resist the pressure to look into the future without looking into the past. We need to be guided back to the pastures of patience, practice, and presence that fill out the substance of the in-breaking kingdom. The primordial habits of the early church are tapping us on our shoulders to gain our attention anew.

In the apostolic letters we observe a movement from *synagogue* to *simple*. The early church went through an awkward but foundational transition. They no longer relied heavily on a brick-and-mortar synagogues as their gathering identity marker. Space was busted open to make room for a new familial temple, made of flesh and constructed by the master builder Jesus. On his second missionary journey the Apostle Paul established the church in Corinth, as related in Acts 18. The city was proud of its political and philosophical environment. The population of the city was cosmopolitan, comprised of Romans and Jews.[10] As this church was being formed the boom of Pentecost was over and the sheen was a bit faded. With synagogue aesthetics and a volume of rituals removed, Jews and Gentiles now had to face each other. New creation was springing up and it looked as delicate as human relationships: simple, beautiful and utterly messy. It was a holy mess but this is garden-variety spirituality—learning the basic agronomy of how to be the people of God in a place. Yet an interruption abruptly occurs to this simple expression. When Christianity gains favoritism within the Constantinian Empire in 312 AD the synagogue forges an appearance again among Jesus-followers. The synagogue begins to shove its way back to the center of Christian identity.[11] The relational plasma steers toward the institutional, the elevated, the visibly exalted, and we've been trying to prop it up ever since to keep it viable. Constantine inaugurated support of Christians, relieving painful persecution but simultaneously pulling up their roots. Moving away from simple uprooted the church and began to disguise

---

9. Hauerwas, *Approaching the End*, 87–88.

10. Gehring, *House Church and Mission*, 92–93.

11. Banks, *Paul's Idea of Community*, 67–68.

its God-given incarnational character. The church in all its success and transitions after 312 AD began to gather up a full garage, attic, and storage shed of clutter. I've been married fifteen years and I know how time and transitions can create a mudslide of stuff being amassed in one's garage. How much more does the church need to seek to declutter? To recover those vintage virtues for the future? To resuscitate our rootedness?

SUBTERRANEAN SEEDLINGS

Building radical churches brimming with radical people begins with recovering the etymology of the word *radical*. We need to salvage the long-forgotten Latin meaning. *Radical* originates from the word *radix,* which means "of roots."[12] Yes, *radical* fundamentally had a meaningful implication of *rooting.* Rooting is the process for cultivating the essential habits, moorings, and functions that ensure long-term relational ecosystem vitality, stability, and resiliency. To be radical is to cultivate deep, deep, deep sustainable roots. Let's call it radical-rootedness. Simplified, radical doesn't go up; it goes down, farther down. There is a current furious flight to radical that needs to be upended. Let's flip radical on its head and plummet it below the surface into rich, messy soil. Instead of transcending the suffering of the world, radical moves us toward the turbulence. A subterranean movement is afoot; a resistance, a rebellion against up, up, and away. The subterranean is a subversive pathway, drawing us downward into more meaningful relationships and a more meaningful way to be the church. We

12. Etymological Dictionary, "Radical."

are to burrow down, rooting deeply and giving opportunity for the kingdom of God to expressly flourish in a distinct place. Nothing has shaped my ecclesiology more than focusing on the smallest, most sacred things. We need a new contentment and aflame affection for being the church below the surface. To be subterranean is to seek a radical-rootedness.

6

Rooting in Fidelity

A TREE IS ANCHORED by roots. Some trees have a taproot amongst their root structures. The taproot is the central root system, from which all other roots sprout. Typically it is thicker and grows directly downward, making it difficult to transplant because it tends to grow so deep that it makes it hard not to break it off in the process of attempting transplantation. The taproot is the chief root, offering the tree and its additional smaller roots significant anchoring and a better chance at growing stronger, longer, and fuller. What is the taproot of rootedness for the kingdom tree? To cultivate *radical-rootedness* we must clarify the indispensable vein running down into the soil and sustaining the preeminent purpose of the Tree of Life. The taproot, like all roots, is subterranean and often not obvious on the landscape for easy viewing. When it comes to a subterranean church seeking a radical-rootedness, the paramount taproot must be identified and we must orient around it, since the tentacles of all other roots stem from it.

What is the taproot for the future of the church?

THE TAPROOT

This primary root is fidelity. Fidelity is the essential character of faithfulness for cultivating a Tree of Life in a place. Fidelity was unequivocally the essential relational marker of the first-century church, as it should be now. I say "relational marker" because fidelity bonded people to each other and to

Jesus. We're in an age where we can skip from idea to idea, easily absconding from difficult situations. Faithfulness was the primary signpost of the saints in Christ; it was the adhesive during seasons of pressure. Revelation 14 speaks of Caesar's fist pressing down to squash early kingdom communities as God's eyes scanned the geography, identifying them by their "patient endurance. . . .[They] keep my ways and remain faithful to Jesus. Blessed are those who remain faithful till the end, for their labor and their deeds will be remembered" (14:12–13). This is the primary root characterizing Jesus' followers. Fidelity is the concept of unfailing loyalty and putting that loyalty into practice, regardless of pressing circumstances. Fidelity exposes our love for what it is, either mere sentimentality or faithful commitment to a long course laden with obstacles. This virtue of fidelity is to be "bound around our neck and written on the tablet of our hearts" (Prov 3:3). Nothing is nobler than the quality to stay and stick when the return on investment is uncertain. I love this quote from Samwise in *The Lord of the Rings*: "You can trust me to stick to you through thick and thin—to the bitter end. But you cannot trust me to let you face trouble alone, and go off without a word. I am your friend, Frodo. Anyway: there it is. We know most of what Gandalf has told you. We know a good deal about the ring. We are horribly afraid—but I am coming with you and following you like a hound."[1] Faithfulness pulls us out of the self into a beautiful surrendered commitment to another. This is the work of love. This virtue has nearly vanished in the contemporary church as the primary way of relating with God and relating to each other.

CRUCIBLE CONDITIONS

As I survey the drama of Scripture, frequently faith is presented at its core, which is our loyalty to the reign of God in Christ. This is the challenge: to be an *alternative people* faithful to the rule of a not-yet-fully-realized kingdom. Maybe it's because we're not a persecuted people that faithfulness is not our primary way of orienting. Whenever there is a little pressure lifted we start to focus on the luxuries, the niceties, the perks, the privileges. It is only natural to outgrow the bare minimum of fidelity when a threat is no longer breathing down our necks. We can observe this dynamic when it comes to eating healthily, the essential bare minimum of nourishing our bodies with vegetables, good fats, and all that other stuff. We have this raunchy, raucous

1. Tolkien, *The Fellowship of the Ring*, 220–21.

bar in our neighborhood that makes the fattest, juiciest burgers. I have literally fantasized about these meaty works of art. So I afford myself the luxury of having one every once in a while. I could lose a few pounds but I don't feel that guilty enjoying one here and there. I know everything would flip the moment I go in for a doctor's appointment if I was having heart palpitations. If I were diagnosed with peripheral artery disease and my wife's big beautiful eyes stared at me in shock, things would get whittled down to the basics pretty quickly. I'd wake up, pitch the juicy burger luxury, and get faithful to eating well. In many ways, *rootedness in fidelity* gets squeezed to the surface under crucible conditions.

The pressure to be faithful expressions of the kingdom of God has not been under duress for the last seventeen centuries. Prior to the Roman emperor Constantine, the early church was nimble, lean, and their alternative social existence was in serious peril. The church had no preferred seat at a political table, no opportunity to be the sexy 501c3 in town, and no affordable comfort to promote their celebrities to the wider world. When Constantine adopted Christianity as the imperial religion, the church became the empire's sidekick.[2] When we no longer need to live on a diet, we have some maneuvering room to fill out a little. Faithfulness is no longer a muscle we need to exercise. When fidelity to the kingdom of God is no longer pressing we may even twist God into a deity fascinated primarily with our personal betterment, making the kingdom a side hobby. Faithfulness to the all-consuming kingdom of God is not birthed in a sterile, sanitized vacuum; its seething enemy is the demands the self makes.

FIDELITY'S ENEMY

The fabric of faithfulness is woven by committing to an entity *outside* oneself. This character of faithfulness can only be born in the mud of wrestling with the ferocious self-oriented ego. The ego is the aspect of the self resolutely concerned with the maintenance of our own wants and wishes.[3] Many of us are taught to invest heavily in our ego, making choices around our preferences, giving fuel to an inner mechanism that wants to absorb all the energy of human relationships for personal consumption or soothing affirmation. It might go undetected but there is a feeding frenzy the ego grumbles for, one of feasting on our own beauty and our own blemishes.

2. Gonzalez, *The Story of Christianity*, 114–15.

3. Zweig, *The Heresy of Self-Love*, 22–23.

The ego wants us to live often and intensely among the mental images of ourselves.[4] This is the narrative akin to the Greek myth of Narcissus, who was unable to express sacrificial faithfulness to anything exterior because of an infatuation with himself. Currently and culturally we are undergoing a revival of this narcissist impulse and the direct collateral death is the virtue of fidelity.

This new narcissism masquerades as neuroses and a low-key misery around the status of our lives.[5] We've convinced ourselves we live with less, never having enough. We don't have enough time, enough money, enough attention, enough emotional energy, enough qualifications, enough experience, enough education, etc. We live with a mentality of need because of the bottomless pit our egos dig for us. This pit is often unnoticeable until you meet someone who does not live this way, who lives as if they have enough. I recently met with a mom and her three kids who were homeless and preparing to sleep in a gymnasium serving as a homeless shelter. I sat on the floor in their little marked-out space in the gymnasium and sought to understand her. She explained how her husband had been abusing her and her kids and they sought escape. She then went on to explain life for her little ones. She shocked me when she shared that nightly she takes the food she receives from a local shelter, attempts to get double portions and then brings it back to her spot in the gym. She then invites others she's met on the street to her small corner and sets up a dinner, parceling out her food to share. She leads them into some normalcy and then she prays for each one's needs around the circle. She explained to me that she felt it was important to be generous to people, offering them some family life even if she was homeless. I was ruined. I assess her life and see so little; she assesses her life and feels grateful: to quote her, "I feel so fortunate to have what I have." Not making light of her abuse, her life is a prophetic poem to us. Even in her survival she is aware and active towards others' needs. Narcissism whispers another narrative: "You don't have enough, you are not acknowledged enough, you are not receiving enough, you have not gotten your dream job yet, you cannot be happy!"

Somewhere deep within we've been convinced that we can fashion an ideal self in the silo of self-consumption. This has become our primary framework for interpreting the world. The ego will challenge any costly commitment that calls us out of the self and into deep enduring sacrifice

4. Ibid, 26.
5. Ibid, 28.

for others. Since faithfulness is a long sacrificial activity for the good of another, it will blow past this as an impediment to self-happiness. This self-orientation wants interior freedom from obligations.[6] The ego is fickle about its passions and might rise up to lend a hand, but when inconvenience is experienced those passions dissolve quickly. This self-possession is tricky enough to pretentiously distort faithfulness into being true to oneself, into a counterfeit faithfulness to individuality, which has a long list of wants that will keep us running errands eternally.

The vision for the kingdom of God is one that counterculturally calls us out of soaking in the self. We are being summoned to commitment and to something costly. Faithfulness requires constant negotiation with the temptation of self-preoccupation that stands stubborn within. This is where the boxing ring is staged, as faithfulness to God's kingdom agenda meets the ravenous fighting ego. We are being invited into an adventure of breaking the egotistical choke hold, rendering it impotent to dominate our lives so that we may give ourselves fully and daily to the movement of God's self-emptying work in the world. Our vision for the kingdom tree is of the utmost importance, summoning all that we are; yet many of our imaginations for being "Christian" place disproportionate emphasis on the self.

OVERDEVELOPING THE PERSONAL

When most people's thoughts of being a Christian are whittled down to its basic idea, Christianity is now understood as a "personal relationship with God"; the image of "God and me" emerges front and center. We are narrowly passionate about our own sense of spirituality, pouring everything about God, the Scriptures, heaven, worship, happiness, missions, etc. through the funnel of the individual connection with God. Taking our own personal spiritual temperature has shaped our imaginations, since being "Christian" is to have things happen "in your heart." We have doused our spiritual language solely in the singular: "my hope," "my sin," "my walk," "my witness." We idolize the just-God-and-me arrangement. Our modern worship songs sound as if it is God's main objective is to intoxicate "me" with his presence. Western Christianity is dizzy on the substance of the "personal." When we speak about faith being personal we tend to think of personal as meaning "applies primarily—or even only—to me," like personal taste.[7]

6. Cohn, *The Pursuit of the Millennium*, 112—13.

7. Hellerman, *When the Church Was a Family*, 69–71.

The sobering truth is that the Bible never uses the word *personal* to speak of God's primary relation to us. When Jesus taught his disciples to pray he did it entirely in plural terms. There are no phrases throughout the entire New Testament like "a personal walk with God" or "a personal relationship with God."[8] The Scriptures do not contain a sustained systematic theological reflection on this concept. It has always haunted me that there is scant biblical support for this but we've made it paramount in our Christian imaginations. The cinder block weight of "personal" has always seemed out of balance with the attention it receives in the New Testament, compelling me to explore where it came from. My suspicion is that modern ideologies and egotism have leaked so heavily onto our theology that they've drowned our idea of God in the soup of the "personal."

The first traces of the vernacular of a "personal relationship with God" appeared in the Great Awakening in the 1730s. Prior to that it's quite difficult to find language like this. The Great Awakening was a revitalization period in church history that made its way through the West, reshaping American conscienceness about God. It's hard to envision religious life in America prior to the Great Awakening because the event thoroughly redefined the way we preach and practice our spirituality today. As much as that season was an awakening it was immersed in the intellectual work of the Age of Enlightenment, which was a cultural thrust that began just before The Great Awakenings.[9] The Enlightenment was started by intellectuals developing the power of reason and individualism to transform society versus the collected corrupt power of institutional tradition. There was a mass swing away from the staleness and deadness of institutions toward the irresistible magic of individualism. Mirroring and baptizing the ideas of the Enlightenment, the Great Awakening piggybacked off the growing individualistic tendencies of an increasingly independence-centered people. Popular preachers such as Jonathan Edwards and George Whitefield justifiably railed against institutionalized versions of church that intellectualized, controlled, and mediated Protestant religious experience. The Great Awakening made Christianity intensely personal to the average pew sitter through the banner message that God wanted to engage each of us individually, "inside your heart." The traditional language for God underwent a progressive morphing during that time as it accommodated to the human craving for connection and intimacy. God's transcendence was losing

8. Ibid., 71–73.
9. Kidd, *The Great Awakening,* 109–10.

audience value but a "personal God" exponentially resonated; to quote a Whitefield sermon: "Jesus is not in heaven, at the right hand of God; he lives in your heart."[10] I'm a big fan of reform and rebellion but there are unintended consequences to every shift. God does love each one of us, but our vernacular for speaking about the faith has become top-heavy and it's tipping over. The blazing center of our God-language is off target. We have been fashioning God in our individualistic image and then reading that concern back into the story of the Bible. Joel J. Miller has pointed out that if you run a Google Ngram on the phrases "personal savior" and "personal relationship with Jesus" they barely exist before the 1970s, at which point they "take off like pair of rockets."[11]

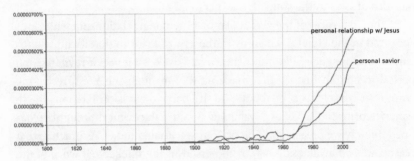

I suspect the mental icon of a "personal relationship" is heavily influenced by the tyranny of the individual-experience economy and less by good hermeneutics. We've synchronized theology with individualistic sensibilities, locating all our speech in this quadrant. We take our sense of hyper-individuality for granted and then assume that is the way God frames self-understanding. God's immanence has squeezed its way to the front and God's transcendence has been relegated to angry preachers preaching an angry potentate. I understand much of the language we use is often a response to the cold-hearted, grumpy deity-judge imbibed at childhood. So the eager search to discover a God that really does love us seems of utmost importance. We long for a divine connection that will soothe the personal pain of our human dislocation.[12] I respect this ache for intimacy, yet in applying therapy to our personal needs we've imported our priorities onto the text, pressing God into a mold that fits our own emotional and

10. Whitefield, "What Think Ye of Christ?"

11. Miller, "Personal Relationship With Jesus."

12. Suk, *Not Sure*, 120–22.

cognitive demands. This is not to say that God does not know each one of us and want us to know him. I do not want to invalidate our experiences. What I do want to call into question is our intensity around "personal." We've overdeveloped this motif and it matters for the future fabric of fidelity in the church. We need to disenthrall ourselves of the conviction that the individual is at the heart of God's plan. De-emphasizing the "personal" is an affront to our insistence to be individually celebrated.

The unintended consequences for God's relation to us being foremost "personal" are that God becomes a utilitarian tool for our self-happiness, self-actualization, and eternal self-security. We look at the Scriptures with a me-prescription lens. It has ruined our Bible reading, causing us to by-pass the first-century authorial intentions. We read passages such as 1 Cor 3:16 as an individualistic, personal promise: "Do you not know that you are God's temple and that God's Spirit dwells in you?" When we come across the pronoun "you" here we assume it means "me" individually, but Paul is *not* describing each believer as their own mini-temple. Instead, "you" is plural—you the "community," together, are God's temple; God's Spirit dwells in you *collectively*. This is not a minor difference or negligible nuance. We read and preach like this all the time, reinforcing a narcissistic, me-centered spirituality. Our personal paradigm for reading the Scriptures must be critiqued and replaced with a social paradigm. Years ago I remember sitting with a grad student after a missionary conference. In the back of the auditorium, we lingered after the last speaker spoke. The student turned and blasted me with words that he'd been holding like a jug full of water in his mouth: "Dan, it's not fair. How come God speaks to that missionary and I've been begging him to speak to me but heard nothing?" His eyes were red and filled with tears. I was saddened by the hyper-personal way this missionary spoke of God with a dynamic of immediate connection we usually associate with in-the-flesh, physical relationships. He spoke as if he cracked the code. It made this young man panic and unintentionally become self-obsessed. Leaders tend to project out their connection with God as the prototype for parishioners, typifying their own temperament as the way to relate to God. We create the impression that God shows up unmistakably every day, leaving many to feel outside the close-to-God club. I grieve that my friend eventually gave up on Christianity but I contend it was because too much weight was placed on the toothpick of the "personal" and it snapped. Basing God's interaction so heavily on individually felt experience makes that relationship precarious whenever a person doubts.[13] Much of our spiritual rhetoric doesn't match our real life with God. We make bold ontological claims that to be a true Christian is to a have real, noetic daily encounter with God, creating a type of mythology around consciousness that receives direct divine voicemail.[14] We proof-text using heroes of the faith who've had unmistakable, sensory-overload intimacy with God but conveniently ignore the masses behind these leaders that missed out. Moses, David, Isaiah, and the Apostle Paul are not templates for a personal relationship. This is not how the Scriptures are to be used and leveraged. In his book *Not Sure*, John Suk explores this tension. "The gospel of John actually wrestles with what the personal absence of Jesus will mean for his followers. 'I am with you for only a short time,' says Jesus, 'and then I go to the one who sent me. You will look for me, but you will not find me; and where I am, you cannot come' (John 7:33–34, 8:21). Jesus shows himself personally to Thomas, but you can almost hear the ache in Jesus' voice when he speaks of us who have not had the sort of personal encounter Thomas did. 'You believe because you have seen'—because, we might say, you have a personal relationship with me. But Jesus goes on to say, 'Blessed are those who have not seen, and yet still follow.'"[15] When we make "personal" fundamental to relating with God, inevitably our faith becomes transactional, not covenantal. When salvation becomes a simple transaction between the individual and God, what God *gives* us will dominate what God is *calling* us into and *fidelity* becomes unnecessary. This is why most attend church for its self-betterment qualities, engage worship as an emotionally energizing exercise, consume liturgies as intellectually stimulating, and have more affection for God as the idyllic friend rather than a King building a Tree of Life in their place.

PROJECTING ONTO GOD

I had a dyed-in-the-wool atheist friend who told me constantly, "Man created God in his own image." Now I certainly don't believe that God is a manufactured fantasy but I do think he was onto something. People have a tendency to project their own desires onto God. In much of Christianity God ironically is concerned first and foremost with being "personal" so that

13. Fitch, *The End of Evangelism*, 91–92.

14. Luhrman, *When God Talks Back,* 113–14.

15. Suk, *Not Sure,* 122–24.

he can take care of me, myself, and I. This God picture is indeed an image of ourselves. God as traditionally understood has become a product of our projected wants and needs. We place God in a "personal box," creating a God who is our own fabrication, embodying our primary values, concerned with our narcissistic whims.[16] When "Christian" is a faith that works for me it is no longer a faith that works for the kingdom of God.[17] We have a tendency to place a mirror between God and us so that we are seeing ourselves. This is the trickery of idolatry.

This explanation of the faith is failing us. I contend that this "personal God" cannot hold up to the harsh elements of doubt, desert seasons, and distracting kingdoms. As one on the precipice, ministering in post-Christian spaces, I see the overly personal way we speak of God backfiring on us. Many become unsettled when they become tuned in to the nagging feeling of God's distance. I know parts of Evangelicalism are still getting mileage out of it, but when personal nearness experiences serious disturbance it begins to unhinge everything else. We are in a crisis of covenant. We have little imagination for relating with God as collective covenant people. Let's be honest, the reign of God in Jesus just doesn't have the emotional zing, it doesn't bring bodies into our modern buildings. But being with Jesus is more than hanging out with spirituality, it's awakening to the royalty of a King. To the first-century Christians, God's reign and self-emptying work

16. Stump and Padgett, eds., *Companion to Science and Christianity*, 170–72.
17. Suk, *Not Sure*, 124–26

to gather the people of God for the good of the world was powerful, emotional, and deeply personal to their collective identity.

UNDERDEVELOPING THE POWERS

In my city we have the joy of being a place for refugee resettlement. Every year the US government relocates people from Burma and the Congo to the north side of our city. Our faith community has developed rich relationships with these survivors of war and poverty. Recently we had a family from an Eastern country over for dinner, to teach us how to cook some indigenous food, then play some board games and share stories. As the sun set and we nursed a good bottle of wine together, our friends shared about life back home. We marveled at their strength as we heard about their creativity, tenacity, and resilience in moving forward. Dead bodies in the streets, people ripped from their homes, and officials conspiring against their prosperity were just a few of the realities that shaped their understanding of power. What popped out to me most was the way they talked about their tribe. The personal groaning for peace was subsumed into the longing for peace for an *entire* people group. The language of "we" was woven throughout. The history of being oppressed by corrupt governments and corrupt empires was deeply embedded in their identity. They suffered with others and told stories from that soreness. They are at war with the Powers and their fields, their homes, their businesses, and their families wait in anticipation of collective relief.

I know nothing of this angle on the world. I don't really have a "people" and I am certainly not oppressed. Here is the conundrum: this is the mold that the New Testament is cast in. This is the vantage point from which every word is articulated. The story of Jesus, the gospel of the kingdom, and a relationship with God is told from the perspective of a people exiled, conquered, and dominated. The Bible is written from this underfoot perspective. I am not part of a first-century-Jewish people living under the Roman sword. So when I read the text of Scripture I read nestled comfortably in my spot of protection and individualistic concerns. The Powers are not a big deal to me and so God takes on my domesticated needs: "what's God's will for my life, what school should I go to, should we make an offer on that home, should we have another kid?" God's word is relatively quiet on matters like these; however, we read Scripture from this perch, disciple people from this privilege, and write worship songs from this romantic angle. God's overturning of the Powers and installing a new Jubilee-kingdom in the now isn't our first way of relating with God. I don't need fidelity to a *kingdom come* when I'm more faithful to *God-and-me*. But following Jesus is more than hanging out with spirituality, it is awakening to the rule of a King.

7

Practicing Fidelity

THE BACKSTORY OF THE arrival of Jesus is that God's people were waiting, longing, aching, grieving, and pleading for God's kingdom to come. The entire Old Testament is jumping up and down prophetically pointing to the arrival of a new King who will usher in a new kingdom in his wake. The Hebrew people's hopes, their peace, their very identity teetered on the arrival of the world's true King.[1] The kingdom of God enacts victory over the Powers that have hijacked the earth. Jesus is the climax of Israel's exhaustive story. We need to be apprentices in this narrative-historical mind-set. Lewis Smedes argues that to be *in Christ* is to be "part of a program as broad as the universe,"[2] as opposed to a narrow, pragmatic, and personal program. The lifeblood of the church in the first century was historically saturated with a kingdom vision of communities laboring for God's new future in the world. Their message of the gospel of the kingdom echoed Moses's announcement to Egypt's Pharaoh that Yahweh was delivering his people and setting them on a renewal mission. A rebellion, a coup, was eventually propelled into the Mediterranean world, seeding a network of faithful church communities under the noses of religious synagogues and pagan empires. These kingdom communities consisting of both Jews and Gentiles, male and female, poor and rich were the concrete social means for expressing the triumph of Jesus.[3] The message of God's all-consuming

1. Wright, *How God Became King*, 83–84.
2. Smedes, *What God Expects*, 110–13.
3. Perriman, *The Future of the People of God*, 77–78.

love was not aimed towards individuals finding a personal friend in Jesus. It was aimed at the invitation to join God's kingdom movement of turning the world upside down (Acts 17:6). To relate with Yahweh is to be rooted in fidelity to a King and the flourishing of his kingdom.

COMPETING EMPIRES

The early church faced many problems, none of them related to not feeling inspired in worship, or the sermon not doing it for me, or the youth ministry not being cool enough for my kids. The battleground was absolute faithfulness to the kingdom of Jesus versus the competing empire of Caesar and its infiltrating ideologies.[4] Fidelity becomes the taproot of relating with God when you're fully aware that opposing Powers are making claims over everyday life. This is how the first-century church understood the cosmos. There are clashing kingdoms at the nexus of the New Testament letters. In the book of Ephesians the Apostle Paul views the present age as dominated by Powers that are in rebellion against God and his purposes for creation.[5] "The power of God raised Christ from the dead and seated him in the place of honor at God's right hand, far above any other king or ruler or dictator or leader. Yes, his honor is far more glorious than that of anyone else either in this world or in the world to come. And God has put all things under his feet and made him the supreme Head of the Kingdom" (Eph 1:20–23). Jesus took a battering ram to the fortress of other gods, busting a hole in their dominance. Evangelicalism has made Jesus so "personal" that he can coexist comfortably alongside powerful ideologies.[6] It is important to exegete Jesus concretely as one historically confronting other lords. This was the vivid imagination of the early kingdom communities gathering on the margins. The Powers sought to prevent shalom, dehumanize people's bodies, and subject people to idolatry. As Christ's resurrection subversively launched alternative communities to live into a new reality there were social patterns seeking to undo loyalty to the upside-down Jesus-kingdom. This is why the taproot of fidelity to the in-breaking kingdom of God was central.

We have a diminished sense of affection for the in-breaking kingdom because we are honed in on the *personal* more than the *Powers*. Our imaginations are being shaped daily by the deluge of Powers convincing

4. Gombis, *The Drama of Ephesians*, 55–56.

5. Ibid., 57.

6. Stassen, *A Thicker Jesus*, 116–117.

us to bend to the commands of consumerism, individualism, Gnosticism, racism, nationalism, etc. But we must stir a new pulsing affection for the kingdom drama that upends and subverts these corrupting Powers in our communities. We need a sociohistorical self-understanding like the first-century church had. The taproot of fidelity is only exercised when we become aware of the force of resistance around us. The subterranean church plays a subversive role in unsettling the evils in this present age, faithfully toiling together for justice, peace, belonging, and healing in our specific locations. We are summoned to gather everything towards this project. We are not idealistic as we live in the tension within the tension of the kingdom come but not yet arrived in its fullness. We do not think in terms of production but in terms of faithfulness. As N. T. Wright notes, "The point is that now the rule of the King of the Jews has been established over the nations and his followers are therefore to go and put that rule into effect."[7]

We ask the question, "What does God want to do in this place?"

What forces seek to undo our faithfulness to the Kingship of Jesus?

THE CHURCH AS RESISTANCE

Rootedness in fidelity is the smoldering axiom for the people of God because this is exactly how God has related to his people from the beginning. Apropos of God's faithfulness to Israel, the prophet heard, "Go, show your love to a woman loved by someone else, who has been unfaithful to you. In the same way the Lord is faithful to the people of Israel, even though they love other gods" (Hos 3:1). God shows love not through sentimentality but through determined fidelity. Nothing screams from the text more than the sometimes seemingly reckless faithful love God directs towards his covenant people. From the fall in Genesis to the Messiah we are exposed to a love that transcends thousands of years of playing-hard-to-get-shenanigans on humanity's part. God is relentless. God does not love by hashtags, sending some pity money, or posting a supportive comment on Facebook. Love is not a onetime act; it's a ridiculous persevering patience. In contrast to the Powers, God does not overpower us with sheer force, production, or showmanship. When Jesus speaks of the kingdom he's not speaking of a

7. Wright, *How God Became King*, 86–87.

political takeover, an armed revolution, an end-of-the-world scenario.[8] We baptize left-wing and right-wing politics all the time and call it kingdom. We are being called into being a community of contrast, not a community engaged in a culture war. The kingdom of God is not shorthand for a "program of social action that will change the world."[9] This was never the vision of the New Testament church, to seek legislation for the expansion of the kingdom. To be rooted in fidelity is to be rooted in the resistance movement of the church, faithful to the mission of being the subversive kingdom presence in the world. Our identity is shaped by our subversive resistance. We do not resist by force or through winning elections. We resist through cross-shaped living. The cross enthrones Christ, which upends every expectation for a larger voice at the table, more status with academic elites, and more adulation from hip blogger critics. The Servant-King calls servant-people into the world as a small, marginalized, decentralized, ordinary, and humble movement. The work of Jesus becomes our creed for the kingdom becoming human. The world is dominated by physical violence and verbal antagonism. I understand it is hard to imagine pushing back the chaos without using the very weapons of antagonistic rhetoric, violence, power grabbing, and a defensive stance in the world. Our church imaginations need a conversion to discern the cross-shaped patterns of life to which God calls his people. A cross-shaped posture is not passive but involves focused vision and sustained reflection on the Servant-King to forge new thought patterns, new ways of hoping, loving, imagining, and behaving. This is not a project in piety, it is a pursuit of living into the kingdom of God for the good of the world and the glory of God. Cultivating communities that take on the cross-shaped posture requires persevering faithfulness to embody a genuine kingdom orientation in the world. We are called to a difficult discipleship of discernment—a nonconformist cruciform faithfulness—that leads to the loss of power but ultimately to a place in God's new heaven and new earth.[10] The is the central task of being the church, "forming active communities made of individuals who pledge allegiance to God alone, who live in nonviolent love toward friends and enemies alike, who leave vengeance to God, and who, by God's Spirit, create mini-cultures of life as alternatives to the empire's culture."[11] This is fidelity; a lifelong communal

8. Perriman, "Mission after Christendom."

9. McKnight, *The King Jesus Gospel*, 89–90.

10. Gorman, *Reading Revelation Responsibly*, 110–11.

11. Hauerwas, *Matthew*, 78–79.

conversion of our imaginations with God's cross-shaped kingdom posture. All of Jesus' life, every ounce of it, was spent on the central aim of launching this faithful people into the world.

When we confess that "Jesus is King," we are confessing that Jesus has say-so in contrast to other competing lesser "kings." There is no Presbyterian God, Anglican God, Methodist God, or Baptist God—there is only one God before whom we all stand.[12] This confession means more than that Jesus is our master. This confession becomes our identity center, giving us a new way to interpret the world.[13] The people of God must always be making sense of their present loyalties in light of the historical narrative offered to us from the early church. Repentance first understood within the New Testament was an ongoing challenge to ideologies that could take over our Jesus-centered ethics and kingdom-directed loyalties.[14] As faithful communities we need to go through an ongoing process of naming and engaging these Powers.

NAMING-AND-ENGAGING MATRIX

Walter Wink sheds light on our human tendency to bow down to lesser lords, which requires a fresh responsibility to name and engage[15] that which seeks to rule over us. I believe subterranean communities should walk through a process of *naming and engaging.* As the Hebrew people were slaves of Powers that dehumanized in Egypt they became dehumanizers themselves as they gained cultural status. It must become an ongoing habit within a kingdom community to submit to the process of naming and engaging lest we begin to coalesce with the Powers themselves.

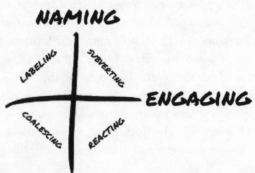

12. Len Sweet, @lensweet, Twitter.

13. Hirsch, *The Forgotten Ways,* 110–11.

14. Trocme, *Jesus and the Nonviolent Revolution,* 120–21.

15. Wink, *Engaging the Powers,* 140–45.

Naming

Naming is a process of identifying forces that seek to woo and wow us into formation. We look beyond the smoke and mirrors to see the real. In conversation in community we seek discernment about the Powers attempting to sabotage our fidelity to the kingdom of God. We name these Powers; we identify them, analyzing their appearances, and articulate how they deceive us in our lives, in our neighborhoods, and in our cities. There are four basic categories for helping us name the Powers as a kingdom community:

- **Ideologies**—a set of conscious and unconscious ideas that seeks to form the basis of one's goals and actions in the world. An ideology becomes a normative vision for seeing all of life.

- **Institutions**—Organized structures or social orders governing the behaviors of individuals within a given community. Institutions mediate the rules on a larger scale.

- **Individual**—a person that holds power in a just or unjust manner.

- **Images**—Objects that cultivate dependence, offering us a sense of worth or escape.

Naming is only half of our practice of fidelity. When we only name we slide into sloppy judgments and apathetic *labeling*. The act of merely labeling can diminish our motivation to application on the ground, convincing us that because we've "named it" we've won. This can merely cultivate an attitude of intellectual enlightenment or a self-righteous posture. Being able to point out a Power must move into localized practices. As James Cone has written, "Indeed our survival and liberation depend upon our recognition of the truth when it is spoken and lived by the people. If we cannot recognize the truth, then it cannot liberate us from untruth. To know the truth is to appropriate it, for it is not mainly reflection and theory. Truth is divine action entering our lives and creating the human action of liberation."[16] Naming is to be done within localized community. The temptation is to merely name Powers through Internet channels of communication. The rage-filled rant has become our convenient cultural outlet against Powers. Tweeting about a justice issue can ultimately relieve the tension of embodied follow-through in practice. When God sent a prophetic witness he didn't send a hashtag—he sent a real-life person in Deborah, Elijah, Hosea, John the Baptist, and Jesus to face real people. I find tossing justice into the winds of

16. Cone, *God of the Oppressed*, 56–57.

the cyber world to be like a pressure relief valve that ironically undercuts feeling accountable to local embodiment. Most seek a national platform for discourse but few seek local embodiment with a voice. The kingdom of God is more than rhetoric. It's quite easy to blast out verbiage online, as it certainly does offer an immediate catharsis. But it does not perpetuate the workings-out of this in the laboratory of flesh-and-blood, eye-to-eye community. Naming within community cultivates integrity with our speech and heads off the creeping hypocrisy the Internet lures us into.

Engaging

Engaging is a process of disarming forces. No wonder Jesus asked, "Why do you call me, 'Lord, Lord,' and do not the things that I say?" (Luke 6:46). It's quite easy to consume the personal God-benefits but not actually resist the Powers throughout the week. As Alice Walker writes, "Anybody can observe the Sabbath, but making it holy surely takes the rest of the week." [17] When Jesus is a hyper-spiritualized savior we will bow down to any appealing king. Engaging is verbalizing our practical resistance. How will we confront the way these named forces creep into our lives to start a coup against King Jesus in our lives? How do we defy and rebel against them? What is my first step in cultivating a new habit in resistance? What sacrifices need to be made? Engaging is often merely reacting when not named within the discernment tank of community. We must think critically and carefully in how we can be "wise as a serpent, gentle as a dove" (Matt 10:16) in engaging the Powers while still living in the empire.

Naming and engaging is one of the primary ways to practice fidelity to the kingdom of God. It moves us into a space of *subverting* the Powers. This is the sweet spot for a community and its inhabitants. Subversion refers to the indirect undermining of established social order and its structures of power. Subversion was a practice often modeled by Jesus. Jesus did this when he highlighted the contrast between God's rule and Caesar's rule. Jesus entered Jerusalem fulfilling Zechariah's prophecy that a king would enter the holy city riding a donkey. "He will cut off the chariot from Ephraim and the war-horse from Jerusalem; and the battle bow shall be cut off, and he shall command peace to the nations" (Zech 9:10) The procession with royal trappings occurred under the tower of the Roman military headquarters, and the subversion could not be missed. Subverting is an alternative to

17. Walker, *In Search of Our Mothers' Gardens*, 103–5.

open belligerency. Jesus also got up the noses of the Temple gatekeepers. It was their job to keep the dirt out of the Temple, enforcing incredibly pervasive purity laws predominantly from the book of Leviticus. Jesus wasn't one for dogma so he physically embodied the new temple when he dined with "sinners" and the marginalized, disputing with the Pharisees over the social boundaries of table fellowship.[18] Jesus models and repudiates class barriers. He leads his disciples to pick and eat grain on the Sabbath, which is a no-no (Mark 2:23).

When we do not walk through the drama of naming and engaging we are unknowingly coalescing with anti-kingdoms. Together let's echo the early church's fidelity in our time, with the same implications, with the same fullness of spirit, subverting our allegiance to anything else but the King and his kingdom. This is not a theoretical spirituality but an ordinary, daily surrendering. The single most fundamental work of the church is to revolt against me-centered ideologies that poison us and cultivate this taproot for the Tree of Life in a real-time place.

18. Myers, *Binding the Strong Man*, 77–79.

8

Rooting in Locality

A FEW YEARS BACK I co-planted a church with a community of friends. We moved into an under-resourced area of the city and we knew we had done something irreversible. We weren't exactly sure how we felt about it either. We had gotten married to a place in our city that was full of pain, prejudice, and poverty, and now we could not get a divorce with our place without losing a big part of our integrity. We'd begun to grasp that the journey of extending the shalom of God would be a long, lifetime work. What had we done? We made vows to a bitterly cold, economically depressed part of the country that is fighting for progress. My wife and I bought a formerly abandoned drug house, gutting it and putting a lot of tender loving care into it. We had multiple families do the same, taking the plunge into this pocket of the city in hopes of extending renewal. The sidewalks were littered with garbage, the roads were peppered with boarded-up houses, the gang violence could make you nervous about going for an evening walk. But now this was our home, this was our place. My wife and I scratched our heads at times, wondering "how the Gehenna did we end up here?" Our neighborhood shaped us. It was a curriculum of sorts, teaching us to be still, listen, absorb, and apply. Not everyone is called to places like this but everyone is called to a place. There is no greater pursuit than cultivating a flourishing community for the renewal of a neighborhood. Before co-planting our church I had moved almost every five years. I'm actually embarrassed by that fact. I confess at times I let opportunities drive my movements. I had been looking for that "thing" but never found it. There was a utopia lingering in my head that I thought existed; a place where everything looked right and worked right. I was an idealist and it soured my commitment towards places. I'm not sure I knew *how* to stay. Since, there has been some surgery in my life exposing my tendency to hover above a place rather than radically rooting myself in it.

Where will you put down roots?

The practice of putting down roots requires something within us to undergo death: "Very truly I say to you, unless a kernel of wheat dies and falls to the ground, it remains only a single seed. But if it does fall into the ground it will produce many seeds" (John 12:24). If our personal career advancement, our personal vocational dreams, our whimsical opportunistic drives do not experience a death on some level, then our lives will not descend into the earthen ground. We will be only one seed. There is a kingdom equation of *being rooted* that when we die to our transience and live for the reign of Jesus in a place, a tree begins to sprout that is bigger than our solo life. The kingdom of God invites us to faithfully submerge into a place. In this work we do not lose our life, we gain it. *Rooting in locality* has changed me and turned me inside out.

GOD IS LOCAL

God is local. His passions and plans for people become concrete when they are localized. Whether it is in the barrenness of the wilderness or the bustling of the city, God has always drawn his people into local places. Starting with the garden, God speaks over the first human community a definitive identity, a banner for self-understanding: "Let us make human beings in our image, make them reflecting our nature so they can be responsible for everything here. . . . So God blessed them telling them to 'enjoy, prosper, be fruitful, fill earth and rule over it.' Then God said, 'I've given you every sort of seed-bearing plant on earth for food. To all animals and all birds, everything that moves and breathes, I give whatever grows out of the ground for food.' And there it was. God looked over everything he had made; it was so good, so very good!" (Gen 1:26–31). It's as if God builds a beautiful housing development with his construction crew and tells the first humans "take care of the place." The Trinity also gives the first human community boundaries, laying out their neighborhood. "A river flows out of Eden to water the garden and from there divides into four rivers. The first is named

Pishon; it flows through Havilah where there is gold. The gold of this land is good. The land is also known for a sweet-scented resin and the onyx stone. The second river is named Gihon; it flows through the land of Cush. The third river is named Hiddekel and flows east of Assyria. The fourth river is the Euphrates" (Gen 2:10–14). Don't zip past this. God limits their responsibility by framing the scope of the garden. They are called to a certain-sized place, a particular location. They are not to go beyond and overreach the location God has situated them in. *Maybe this feels frustrating? Maybe they want to be bigger than the neighborhood garden? Maybe this is part of the reason they ate of the apple?* When we do not embrace the finite space we're bound to we inevitably neglect the space we inhabit. We will not fill our neighborhood with maximum listening, life, and love. Our attention spans are elsewhere. In Genesis, God is pulling on the attention of the first human community saying "look, this is your neighborhood, it's wild and wonderful—revel in it!" The first human community's self-understanding will be intertwined with the micro-space of the garden. *Who* they are is also *where* they are. God's original intention is that the blueprint for being human is to orbit and tend to the details of a place. The Maker puts into his gloriously created project the DNA of "progressive generativity," meaning that everything is built to grow.[1] This created place is going somewhere. This work of art is not static or idle. God makes things that move, create, and expand. This is important to understand about the nature of place. For as firm and fixed as a place might appear on the surface it is soft and adapting underneath. When God said the place was "very good" he did not mean it was finished or perfect. There was work still to be done as the place had a wild atmosphere. God charged Adam and Eve to care for and cultivate the Genesis-era world; the first humans were a "place-based" community. God continues prescribing this blueprint of human self-understanding even after the fall in Genesis 3. The Hebrews were enslaved in Egypt but were eventually rescued *for* the cultivation of a place and given intricate designer details recorded in Leviticus on how to merge proactively and peacefully with their new location. Their act of worship was rooted in how they *cared for* and tended to their place.

---

1. Fretheim, *Creation Untamed*, 36–37.

IDENTIFIED BY A PLACE

The kingdom of God has no other orientation than one that gets particular by manifesting in the local. The kingdom of God is not an esoteric concept or an abstract ideal brewed up in the academy. Being rooted in locality is how the early church was identified. The first Jesus communities were anchored in a geographic self-understanding. Early Christian communities were identified by their location, clearly noticeable as Paul greets church's meeting in a particular home grafted to a particular place. He tells the community in Thessalonica to "live quietly in their place, and work with their hands in order that they may earn the respect of those who don't yet believe Jesus is the Messiah" (1 Thess 4:12). This is the way Paul continuously addresses and identifies churches; as a gathered people in a specific part of the city. This may not seem so profound until you contrast it with the way we identify churches today by denominational beliefs, styles of worship, and branded personalities. The missional church of the future must resurrect, reemphasize, and reorient around a full subterranean dive into place, being rooted in locality. When our big church personalities eclipse love of neighbor, we cash out the character of the church.

The local space is where all things come to collide. It is where all our wish-dreams must work with the existing people and resources in a neighborhood. Being rooted in locality calls us to open our eyes to what is already present there, to behold the weight of our neighbors' glory, as C. S. Lewis has so eloquently stated.[2] In farming this is called bricolage, which is the fine art of constructing something new out of the valuable existing matter already available in a place. We must acknowledge that God's dwelling is already tied to the neighborhood, the streets connecting us to each other, the homes we eat in and the parks that we play in.[3] God has not been waiting on pins and needles for our arrival. The relational ecosystem in our neighborhoods already has a hearty amount of the material needed for the creation of something beautiful for the kingdom of God. Abundance is already in the arteries of our neighborhoods. There is a labyrinth of life and culture that must be recognized and respected. We must resist the urge to treat our city like a campaign of war and rather see it as a garden of stories to sit with and tend to. Our first orientation as a church must be to look,

2. Lewis, *The Weight of Glory*, 3–19.
3. Wilson-Hartgrove, *The Wisdom of Stability*, 32–34.

listen, and learn.[4] *What is here? Who is here?* My neighborhood invites me to gain eyes of faith for holy interruptions and for blips on the radar of meaning. People are not ideologues, propaganda pieces, or pawns for our plans, they are just people. We must denounce treating people as means to our ends. We must avoid the trap of having good intentions for others, but using manipulative means to "arrive."[5] The future of the church is in the stripping away of all gimmicks in order to dwell in a place with the flesh-and-blood people living there. This is where the kingdom tree will sprout up from roots cultivated deep below the ground. So, first seek to root deeply in a place. Jesus moved unassumingly into Nazareth and this was no menial part of the plan. Before Jesus died on a cross he was present in a neighborhood. It was the way in which God forever modeled for us how to be where we are.

NOT ENOUGH TO GO AROUND

We have natural propensity to zone in on scarcity, to zero in on lack. Scarcity is a mental and emotional life framework that "we do not have enough" of something—enough time, enough money, enough education, enough leaders, enough energy, or enough strength. We believe we have too little, and the psychic cost is that we see deprivation before we see abundance. When it comes to having eyes for the neighborhood we allow scarcity to colonize our minds. "Scarcity captures the mind," explains Sendhil Mullainathan. "It promotes tunnel vision, focusing us purely at crisis but making us less insightful, less forward-thinking, less wise long-term"[6] Christians tend to see what is broken before what is beautiful. We are not sure how to acknowledge, celebrate, and honor what is good and fruitful when we see so much need or deprivation.

Christ taught us to gain eyes to see and ears to hear abundance rather than scarcity first. Many see the miracle in which Jesus divided the fish and loaves as a lesson on divinity fixing a problem of hunger; however, there is more to the scene. The story offers an image of a God of abundance, which seems to contradict everyday impressions that scarcity besets the world. God's love and faithfulness is limitless. This is why Jesus so often said, "Fear not," even though his disciples lived in a world in which there seemed to

---

4. Schreiter, *Constructing Local Theologies*, 88–90.

5. Lupton, *Toxic Charity*, 74–75.

6. Mullainathan, *Scarcity*, 55–56.

be pervasive scarcity and violence. I have a hard time believing that at the miracle of the feeding of 5,000, that many people traveled a great distance and forgot to bring food. However, I believe as time wore on, many people's supplies started to dwindle. I suppose that many in the crowd felt scarcity rather than abundance, becoming stingy in sharing with those who had not prepared well for the day. A young boy offers his loaves of bread and fishes and a miracle is sparked. Children are more wide-eyed, more trusting, and less cynical. I think this story illustrates a mind-set of scarcity that people dwell in that prevents them from living in abundance like children; "whoever does not receive the kingdom of God like a child shall not enter it" (Mark 10:15). It is difficult for us to avoid thinking in terms of scarcity, since notions of scarcity are all around us. Even though we may not say it with our mouth we act as if God is limited in love and generosity. We feel purely defined by our original sin. In the garden of Eden, Adam and Eve believed they did not have enough and that they needed more. This attitude also led to Cain's murder of Abel, in which Cain assessed his resources and thought "I can't spare that much, I don't have enough to give away." Abel believed in God's abundance, God's daily bread. The people of God in the desert were given an abundance of manna but they demanded meat. Scarcity seeps into our ability to engage our neighborhood as ones seeing how the kingdom of God is already breaking in. I think our scarcity mentality is culturally conditioned but I also connect it to the way we describe God. Many of the ways we describe God are in terms of the negative, explaining God by what God is not. This way of orienting our God language comes from apophatic theology, also known as negative theology.[7] It's a theological lens that attempts to describe God primarily in the context of what he's not. Negative theology played an important role early in the history of Christianity. Three theologians who emphasized the importance of a negative theology of God were Gregory the Theologian, John Chrysostom, and Basil the Great.[8] The argument goes that because God is transcendent we do not know God on God's terms. The only way to explain God is describe him in the opposite terms of humans. Few would accept the label "apophatic" in their theology but I'm convinced this sentiment has infiltrated our sensibilities about how God relates with the world, as one identifying what's bad about the world in contrast to himself. This gives us an imagination for what God is not but not for what God is. Certainly as Jesus journeyed about the Ancient

7. Boesel and Keller, eds., *Apophatic Bodies*, 145–46.
8. Ibid., 147–48.

Near East unwrapping the kingdom of God in word and deed he labeled what was broken but he also ushered in a new lens for seeing that "the kingdom of God doesn't come by counting the days on the calendar. Nor when someone says, 'Look here!' or, 'There it is!' Because God's kingdom is already among you" (Luke 17:21). Seeing abundance when scarcity seems ubiquitous is difficult but it is an essential starting point for participating in God's redemption of the world.

Years ago this was a new orientation for me. When I thought about church I first thought about what we could add to the ingredients that would attract or would be the solution to a problem. Could we put something or someone on the stage, or could we mix something into the stew of a program that would compel someone to come check us out? This is a performance-based lens, not a presence-based lens.

WEAKNESS IN THE NEIGHBORHOOD

When we saturate our understanding of being the church in the sacred but small space of a neighborhood we will be humbled. Humility comes from the word *humiliation*. Humiliation casts a picture of people snickering and noticing your shame. Superseding our limits tells us to go where we are strong, not where we are noticeably weak. Most drift the church has experienced is a movement away from a radical local orientation, which is a movement away from humility. It is a bad missional practice to bring in the shock-and-awe campaign of money, projector screens, expertly trained musicians, and all the trimmings to be missional in a place. Resist the urge to bring in the professional artillery for mission. When we attempt to build the church like it's an arms race we will feel weak and exposed. The sheer complexity of the personal lives and systems in a neighborhood can do an angry dance on your pride. The neighborhood will humble your brilliant ideas formed in academia, your skills refined in leadership school, and your opinions lifted from a bookshelf. The neighborhood is full of heat that will burn up your ego. *Is this a good thing?* Yes. Everything in our culture tells us to avoid weakness like a car swerves around a pothole. A voice is screaming at us from all corners of the world to appear strong, slick, and secure in our spiritual standing. So my hunch is that we have the tendency to create spiritual environments where we can control the spiritual temperature and reception. This builds churches that may be located at a street address but may not be present in a place. We may have a sign out in front of the building but not be saturated in the relational ecosystem of our city. Presence will call us to deconstruct the plethora of activity produced in our church buildings in order to move people to reorient around the brokenness in their neighborhood. If the church does not warm up to this redirection, gradually it will no longer be present in the world; it will have just created its own spiritual compound. The church does not need to appear as the strongest entity on the block; rather it should appear as the most readily accessible community on the block.

TENTING TO TABERNACLING

Jesus stepped into the pothole of weakness. Embracing weakness starts by stepping into the way people receive us, understand us, and relate with us. Choosing to root in a local space will position you to feel the blunt force of human interaction. We cannot control the neighborhood. Presence is the currency of the street and if we shortcut real-time presence we avoid taking the path Jesus took. Our own weakness in a place is an instrument God uses to birth the beauty of Christ's own presence in a place, an unrelenting delivery of the love of God into the lives of others.[9] "If you've gotten anything at all out of following Christ . . . then do me a favor and see yourselves the way Christ Jesus thought of himself. He had equal status with God but didn't think so much of himself that he had to cling to the advantages of that status. He set aside the privileges of his position and took on a much lower status becoming human. Having become human, he lived the human existence, allowing it to humble him. He didn't claim special privileges. Instead, he lived a selfless, obedient life and then died a selfless, obedient death" (Phil 2:5–8). The process of missional living humbled Christ as he was subjected to the limitations of being with people. God has been moving toward people throughout the entire scope of the Scriptures.[10] Human weakness subjected Christ to pain as he stepped towards people rather than away from them. The Apostle Paul speaks of his vulnerability in spending time with the people in the city of Corinth: "I came to you in weakness, fear and much trembling when I spent time with you" (1 Cor 2:3). To shed all the armor to be with people in our place is submitting to the way in which Jesus came to us. This is how we share in his weakness. The arc of the Scriptures is one of downward humility. As an introvert I've had the

9. Yoder, *Theology of Mission*, 130–33.
10. Herbst and Lyons, *Where You Live Matters*, 23–24.

tendency to believe that it is in the desert by myself that humility will be formed. As I navigate the silence, contemplating God's voice in my life I do come to see my own need for humility. Yet I'm even more convinced it is in the fire of being with other people, warts and all, that melts our egos, our sense of control, and our clichéd answers formed in classrooms. I can easily think I'm humble in the silo space of my monastic mind, but faced with the sheer prickliness of people I'm invited into real formation. I'm faced with the more excellent way of love.

As we see in Abraham and in his family they were in a place of suspension, not yet rooting. "By faith Abraham, when called to go to a place he obeyed and went. He made his home in the Promised Land like a stranger in a foreign country; he lived in tents, as did Isaac and Jacob, who were heirs with him of the same promise. For he was looking forward to the city with foundations, whose architect and builder is God" (Heb 11:8–10). This passage is alluding to a transition of where God's activity is. Abraham was not yet rooting, he was tenting in a place. But Jesus makes the transition for us that we could not make ourselves; he takes the *tenting* of the people of God and grounds it—"The Word became flesh and made his dwelling place among us. We have seen his glory, the glory of the one and only Son, who came from the Father, full of grace and truth" (John 1:14). The word *dwell* in this text is in Greek *episkenoo* or "to tabernacle." This movement of *tabernacling* was the plan all along as begun in Genesis—for God to dwell in the neighborhood of the world, to reside, to make a home in a rich and full way. Jesus carried the quest of Abraham and rooted it to this world, to this place. Yet notice this tabernacling did not land in a pillar of fire and in an untouchable personality. This tabernacling appears in weakness, in an uncomfortable frailty. When God comes to dwell in the neighborhood in the fleshy body of Jesus he does not come in what human civilizations would call magnificence; he comes with an unimpressive meekness.[11] The God of the cosmos has the ability to be wounded and rejected. We extend the incarnation of God into the neighborhood when we imitate Jesus' approach to mission. The humble incarnation of Christ is not yet completed as the church is called to "complete what is lacking in Christ's afflictions" (Col 1:24). As we die to our attempts to use power and prestige to accomplish God's purposes in the world we enact the foolishness of the cross (Gal 2:19–20). This is a cross-shaped method for mission. Being cross-shaped calls us not to hide our weaknesses, inadequacies, and failures but to fend

11. Dawn, *Powers, Weakness, and the Tabernacling of God*, 59–61.

off self-promotion and the trumpeting of our strengths. God's invitation to tabernacling calls us away from ultra-competence into humble-presence.[12] I'm convinced the greatest gift the church can offer the world is *not* a highlight reel of our best preaching and worship performances. As we root in the neighborhood we refuse to try to control what people think of us or to cultivate a desired image. Jesus' suffering has left us an example of how to walk gently, humbly, and with perseverance in our places. We don't just learn abstract ideas of the the cross from the Scriptures, we are summoned to reenact them as a way of life for following Jesus into the guts of the world. The energy of the incarnation is moving us from tenting to tabernacling. When God fills the bones of the human Jesus it begins God's campaign to root locally in the world.

As we begin to accept the scandalous and sacred call for the church to reorient around the neighborhood the hope of being locally rooted will fill us with vision, but we must not wear rose-colored glasses. The moment you invite and challenge people to move towards being rooted in locality is the moment you feel the consternation. For as much as wonder can fill our imaginations, something resists within us. Something gripes and groans in our conscience when we finally get around to application. In my own work of rooting and discipling others into a subterranean way of life we unearth what social scientists call the displacement effect.

DEALING WITH DISPLACEMENT

In 2005 I spent some time in Kenyan refugee camps. The refugees there were from Uganda and had been uprooted as they fled from the Lord's Resistance Army. The formation of the rebel group called the Lord's Resistance Army (LRA) recruited 5,000 children into the Ugandan government army. The LRA has been accused of widespread human rights violations, including murder, abduction, mutilation, child sex slavery, and forcing children into hostilities. My role was to explore not the LRA itself but the issues related to attachment by families that resettled in Kenya. As we visited these refugee camps we compiled information and stories about the serious struggle for individuals and families to attach to a new place indefinitely. The issue we investigated was called the displacement effect. The displacement effect names the influence that an extended season of uprootedness has on rooting. When people are put out of home, of place, and hover in a

12. Ibid., 66.

displaced state, it creates a settlement identity crisis.[13] When the emotional muscle of attachment is suspended or underdeveloped it makes attachment significantly difficult. It is often an unconscious psychological state that makes place attachment feel threatening, constricting, unfamiliar, frightening, or temporary.

My wife and I have been working toward adoption for awhile. In our training over the years we've learned much about displacement and attachment challenges that a toddler might experience coming into our home. Our tiny one may resist and potentially sabotage attachment because of a previous inconsistent history with forming bonds. When there is prolonged separation we form self-reliance. In both of these scenarios I am awed by the human spirit to survive despite being uprooted, yet it is evident that the work of recovering a healthy *self* is to embark on a journey to greater rootedness.

This exploration has made me acutely aware of the signs of the displacement effect.[14] In no way do I want to minimize my previous examples of displacement, but I do think we are experiencing a version of displacement in the affluent West. Coming to terms with how displaced many of us are is imperative for the future of mission. Given our postmodern and poststructuralist turn, there is a strong orientation towards multidimensionality, taking a more pluralistic approach to identifying with a place. This means we are spread thinner, with lesser depth in any one place. We envision ourselves as more connected globally with less loyalty locally. This has made us more world-wise as we are connected to multiple places, but this cultural force has also made us less emotionally bonded to one neighborhood, accumulating violence against our ability to stay and sink in. Atrophy has settled into our muscles needed for rooting. Our attachment to location has been disrupted and it has severe psychological consequences for our society.[15] Even with all our progress as a civilization, we are experiencing social disintegration. Finding people that choose to settle deeply, fending off transience, might seem like an artifact. The future of the church must model a contour of resistance to be the people of God in a place.

Transience is a by-product of a combination of factors: the rite of passage of going away to college, additional graduate-level education, shifting economic opportunities, chasing the American dream, and unstable

13. Feldman, "Settlement Identity," 78–79.

14. Fenichel, *The Psychoanalytic Theory of Neurosis*, 92–93.

15. Apfelbaum, "Memory and Dislocation," 108–9.

homelife situations. Six out of ten[16] people interviewed by the Pew Research Center said they may move in the next five years. Asked why they live where they do, movers most often cite the pull of economic opportunity. Stayers most often cite the tug of family and connections. Being rooted in locality is much more than staying put in one place, but it does include that. It is hard to be intentional about presence when you're passing through. The call to stability and intentional rooting in a place is a countercultural invitation. Rather than financial opportunity driving our decisions, what would it look like for kingdom rooting to be the guideline in our decision-making? Rooting is relating and relating takes invested time.

Our *lifeworld*, a term coined by David Seamon, is the place our bodies dwell; it is a human-scaled environment to which we are integrally limited.[17] Our bodies, with our senses, our touch, our eyesight, our footprint, and our abode-making can only be in one place. We are increasingly taking this smaller world for granted, allowing it to go unnoticed and neglected. A gritty sci-fi movie titled *Surrogates* illustrates this well. It takes place in the year 2017 and humans live in near-total isolation, rarely leaving the safety and comfort of their homes, thanks to remote-controlled robotic bodies that serve as "surrogates," designed as better-looking versions of their human operators. Daily, people lie down in pods and go online to live through their surrogate selves in the world. Because the damage done to a surrogate is not felt by its owner, it is a peaceful world free from fear, pain, and crime. This movie hints at the parallels to our increasingly detached existence. We shelter and insulate ourselves from our real-time places. Something is distorted when we get enraged with statements made on the Internet but barely feel the pains of our own neighborhood. We know how to build compelling structures but we fear beholding a neighborhood. We know how to consume the entertainment perks in a place but don't know how to identify with the pains in a place. We are tasked with reversing this trend as the church of the future.

DISCIPLESHIP TOWARDS LOCALITY

This is ultimately the work of discipleship: inviting people on a journey that no longer sees their neighborhood as a prop in the background. The discipling work is an unlearning and relearning how to be in a place; moving

16. Desilver, "How Polarized Americans Live Differently."

17. Seamon, *A Geography of the Lifeworld*, 45–47.

from haphazardness to intentionality; cultivating place-sustaining interactions rather than place-undermining interactions.

How do we go about becoming a neighborhood?

How do we shift our habitual patterns towards attachment?

In place attachment theory this is called elective attachment.[18] We need a new metaphor for discipleship that tilts us and upends us into the rich soil of our neighborhoods. Discipleship should echo the framing and commissioning given to the first human community. We come full circle from the call upon Adam and Eve's lives to be intertwined with the micro-space of the garden. God's original intention is that the blueprint for being human is to center on and tend to the details of a place. Our shaping as apprentices of Jesus happens as we merge together the historical creation narrative and the new creation future to create a present practice. Before we get into some practical tools for rooting in locality in our next chapter we must set up a geographic-tinged metaphor for discipleship. The metaphor I find most helpful is *the garden, the gardening, and the gardeners.*

The Garden—Seeing Neighborhoods

God got really clear about his love for the world by moving into the Nazareth neighborhood. We need to get clear about locality. Like a raised bed in a garden box, we need to define the size, shape, and contents of our garden. Your garden may be a section of your city or include several small towns in your county. If the language you use in your church is always connected to the brick and mortar of your Sunday gathering place, then you will naturally count heads as the means to measuring. Rather than talking about the neighborhood, you talk about building your church. Direct eyes outward. Pull people out into the garden to explore, to behold, to understand where they live. Release into the air imagination for the particular locale God has situated your community in. Make it obvious over and over that the energy is outside the building in the neighborhood. This takes a lot of bandwidth, but it is the most foundational rooted shift. Moving people's affections beyond the spiritual goods and services they consume to the needs in their neighborhood is moving from a "me" orientation to mission orientation. Honestly there is probably nothing more vital or volatile than this work.

18. Manzo and Deveine-Wright, *Place Attachment*, 78–82.

Consider:

- Who is in our city?
- Who are our neighbors?
- Where do we live?
- Who is already doing good work in this garden?
- What is beauty and brokenness in our place?

The Gardening—Seeding Relationships

It's not enough to have increased intelligence of a neighborhood; we need better relational attachment. Cultivating a garden is more than raising money for an initiative or throwing in some skilled leaders. The garden needs us to get on our hands and knees and enjoy the soil. Is your church relationally investing in a region? We need to move beyond an event mind-set to a rhythm mind-set. Having events that catalyze serving in our city can cause good sparks. Those sparks can easily be compartmentalized. Our passion must be sustainability. We must cross and close the relationship gap. We must push for tangibility about how to foster connectivity with a place. This is the labor of incarnation. Create spaces for clusters within your church to brainstorm the pathways into a particular place. Let people verbalize their challenges, ideals, fears, and hurdles to bridging the relational disparities with their neighbors.

Consider:

- How are we going get dirty in our place?
- On a daily basis?
- On a weekly basis?
- On a monthly basis?
- On a yearly basis?
- How can we do this in micro-groups? With other families? With our friends?

The Gardeners—Shaping Disciples

I've had a urban garden for a few years. My wife is the expert and must continually teach me how to plant seeds and nurture them to life. She understands the conditions of the soil and the variables of gardening. I've got a lot to learn. Every spring, that garden needs fresh work and focus. *If you're inviting people to into the garden how will you equip them? How will you foster their intelligence and their perseverance?* Gardeners burn out without nourishment and best practices. How do we build a disciple culture? Tilling and toiling require tools. What tools are you putting in the hands of your gardeners? Gardeners who inhabit a relational ecosystem will need sustenance to continue. Jesus will build the church if we make disciples. Shaping disciples is not directed at more service to the church infrastructure but more service to the labyrinth outside our church doors.

Consider:

- How are we cultivating disciples?

- How are we training for the hands-on work of missional dwelling?

- How are we clearing out space on our church calendars for this work?

9

Practicing Locality

THIS CHAPTER IS BROKEN up into two locality guides meant to help aid and empower practice for disciples. The first is a foundational guide, the *renewal tool* for an entire community to embrace and enact. The second guide is a *submerge tool* for individual disciples to help them reorient towards a schema for rootedness where they live. This tool assists communities and individuals in their journey from *detachment* to *attachment* in their places.

RENEWAL TOOL

The renewal tool has four quadrants that are organized into two halves. The bottom half is *incarnation,* grounding us in real-life faithful presence, with real people in a particular place. Incarnation resists forming idealized plans from a classroom. Incarnation is the means of learning how to be somewhere physical with kindness, humility, faithfulness, and self-control for the sake of leaning into the renewal of all things (Rom 8:19–21). *Imagination* is the top half of the tool. Imagination is where we envision the future promises of God being worked for in the present. We allow the Spirit in our community to inspire us to see clearly, discern carefully, and create boldly. As we move through the flow of renewal we will move from *Interaction* to *Interpretation* to *Innovation* to *Improvisation.* This shaping missional process does not cease, although we must seek to submit to it. As long as we are staying put in a place we must be journeying slowly through this formational flow of renewal.

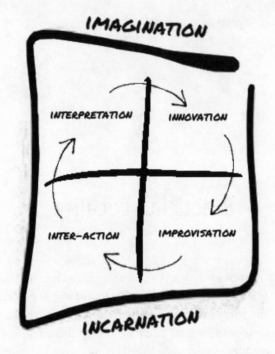

Adapted from IDEO's Innovation Process

Incarnation

Incarnation is where theological rubber meets the road. It is the space where our bodies and our beliefs meet. If theology does not inform how we embody in a particular place it is not real theology but rather an empty ideology. Our theology of God in Christ should speak to the realities that mark our lives together. One of Augustine's most basic insights was that Christian theology was confession of two things: a confession of *who God is* with our mouths and a confession of *who we are* with our bodies.[1] You can tell a lot about a church's theology of God by where it spends most of its time, money, and energy. If you spend most of your human resources in spaces that attract and extract people out of the world then the primary image of God you project is one of God is still residing far above "place." Certainly this is a view of God we have in our Bibles, but it is a transitional one. Defining the character of God using the Old Testament is like jumping to conclusions in the middle of a conversation. Jesus is the completion

1. Augustine, *The Confessions of St. Augustine*, 35.

of the conversation, permanently transitioning how we see who God is, where God is, and how God will be identified. Our theology must reflect the bodily realities of day-to-day life in a neighborhood because when God filled out theology for human understanding it was poured into the body of a living, breathing, eating person in a real town. Christ believed, at the core of his being, that it was his destiny and vocation to bring God's love deeper into the world through his own embodied pain and perseverance. The Word became flesh to reveal that words alone cannot witness to the in-breaking kingdom. Jesus subjected his body to humanity as he was representing humanity to God.[2] This is how God was and is revealed. When the Father sent the Son, Jesus left the glory of his Trinitarian abode and became a helpless infant in the care of humans. Jesus grew up and became a first-century sandal-sporting, temple-frequenting Jew. He accommodated first-century Jewish culture and immersed in the lifeworld of a town. Being *incarnational* is more than wearing relevant attire; it demands humility of heart to listen to the stories of others, to empathize with their frustration, suffering, and brokenness. As Isaiah says, "all flesh shall see it together" (Isa 40:5). Our theology of God cannot be abstract and dehistoricized, which often can happen in more systematic theologies. When Jesus becomes a doctrine rather than a living theology of being in a place we mute and tame his influence on us. Jesus is theology in the flesh. We can become *deformed* by our doctrines if they are not shaping us to root deeply with intention in a neighborhood. We can however become *reformed* in our bodies by the process of faithful incarnational presence.[3] We cannot be a theologically rich people without being radically rooted and refashioned around incarnation. Incarnation is the slow process teaching us to how to be patient, resisting agitated action. To do theology faithfully, we must participate in the social realities of our broken and beautiful places.

Interaction

Interaction is the long, out-in-the-streets process of finding meaningful relational exchanges with the lifeworld of a place. The first ongoing practice for a community of disciples is to seek genuine *interaction* with a neighborhood. Living theology is an interactive process that is both conversational and contextual, in which we are being formed by our local place and

2. Athanasius, *On the Incarnation*, 32–33.
3. Yoder, *Theology of Mission*, 112–14.

forming it by our presence. Interaction compels us not to organize interaction on our turf, inside our buildings with our professionals at the podium, but rather to push our community out into the wild garden of our city. We must teach our bodies to dwell in a location from which we seek to understand, hear, and simply see how others live in the same lifeworld we inhabit. We should seek to interact with our lifeworld's hopeful celebrations: its joys, its pains of oppression, and the violence it feels. We speak from *where* our bodies are situated. Too much theologizing and Christian living techniques are formed in the ivory tower of the Christian world, telling us what people need and how they should receive it. This is presumptuous and prideful. This is what happens when information is divorced from immersive interaction. Our theological speech should not flow from a protected place but from embodied life with our neighbors. There is no such thing as a distinction between us and the world. We are made from the dust of the ground and the particles of our cities permeate us all. Too many gain their information about humanity from cable news, allowing it to characterize who people are, creating a chasm of antagonism. My own community has collectively sought to practice *interaction* by being at our neighborhood's multicultural festivals, block parties, and neighborhood meetings. Our city hosts a beautiful parade that celebrates the diverse refugee population that has settled here. We see it as a vital interaction to go, volunteer, and be present. We've participated in weekend neighborhood snow shoveling with other neighborhood organizers, resisting slumlords that don't take care of their own snow build-up. Recently I had a friend's mostly Caucasian community be present at an African American-organized march against violence, not seeking a pat on the back but seeking solidarity. Find ways to interact. Never look at this as "doing the dishes." This is no menial ministry. It in we weave ourselves into the fabric of our place, enmeshing in interconnected ways. Interaction is an effort in humanizing our neighbors, hoping to regain a familiarity with their lifeworld filled with touch and sound. These become reciprocal relationships, a two-way street in which we are changed and transformed in the relationship.[4]

Interaction must ask:

- What is happening in our neighborhood?

- What are people celebrating and how do we participate?

- What are people grieving and how do we participate?

4. Roxburgh, *Missional*, 98–101.

- What are people creating and how do we participate?
- How do we make space to join the rhythms of our neighborhood?

Interpretation

We then move to the process of interpretation. This is not strictly a linear process, although occasionally it can be. Interpretation flows out of the patient embodied time we've spent in interaction. I cannot stress enough how slowness must be embraced in this season. Efficiency culture pressures us to blaze through interaction quickly so that we can get to the results stage. Interpretation is vital in incarnational renewal. As a community we must interpret what we are seeing and what we are seeing in ourselves. This is a healthy discipleship tension to cultivate. In seeing people clearly we must allow ourselves to be interpreted. At one point Jesus performs an odd two-stage miracle. Jesus spits in some dirt, makes some mud from the ground, and puts it on a blind man's eyes. Then the blind man says, "I see people; they look like trees walking around." Once more Jesus put his hands on the man's eyes. Then his eyes were opened, his sight was restored, and he saw everything clearly (Mark 8:24–25). At first the man's vision was hazy. Only when Jesus touches him a second time can he see clearly. What is going on here? Was Jesus losing his miracle mojo? I think not. Early in the text Jesus warned his disciples to beware of the leaven of the Pharisees (Mark 8:15). *Leaven* is a word for the yeast necessary for baking bread, but in this case it refers metaphorically to the bankrupt teaching of the Pharisees. The disciples scratched their heads and wondered why Jesus was talking about literal bread. Jesus got seriously upset and responded, "Don't you have eyes can you not see, don't you have ears can you not hear?" (Mark 8:18). Jesus is genuinely aghast that his disciples have spent so much time with him but still blind to what the kingdom of God is doing.[5] Maybe they are so steeped in information about the Torah that they cannot see past their doctrines. Jesus makes a statement with the healing of this blind man that even though we may have encountered Christ we still have a case of nearsightedness to some degree or another. Our own bloated theological knowledge packs our corneas full of information, smudging up our vision. We are like the blind man who has been made to see but even in our sight we do not see clearly the images before us. We must take a teachable pos-

5. Wright, *Mark for Everyone*, 89.

ture as we are confronted by our ignorance and misplaced judgments. We must recognize our own blindness and limitations in the spaces we dwell in. We must *behold*, not just *look*. To behold is to look beyond the surface of what we see and also look beyond the immediacy of our own trite answers. In interpretation we hold the fleeting images in our minds and feelings in our heart and freeze them for assessment.[6]

As we interpret we ask about ourselves:

- When did I feel disgust?
- When did I feel anger?
- When did I think, "get over it"?
- When did I think, "this is dumb"?
- When did I feel unlove?

As we interpret we ask about others:

- What are we seeing?
- What power dynamics are we observing?
- Who is doing good work in this place already?
- Who is being marginalized?
- Who are the influencers here?

Innovation

New possibilities are opened up when we move through the immersive incarnational practice of interacting and interpreting. We journey into the space of innovation. Innovation is birthed when new clusters of people collide with local realities, emerging with a fresh approach. It is in the human genome to get creative when faced with problems we're immersed in. This is a healthy impulse, yet as with any healthy impulse it can be destructive if it becomes competitive, especially in light of the kingdom of God. When innovating an idea for planting seeds of the kingdom tree in a neighborhood we should seek out partnerships with others outside our micro-community. Empire building has become the reputation for too many Christian communities. In naiveté we say "nobody is doing ministry here." There are certainly cracks and crevices in our neighborhood that

---

6. Paul, *God in the Alley*, 44–46.

others are not pressing into. It is good and necessary to move into them. There will always be leaders and churches that want their names branded on innovations. Those with money and resources can create an innovation bureaucracy because of their privilege. If you have money and manpower this can actually make you bulldoze over others' work. Instead, seek to have your innovations walk gently and quietly so as to not stomp all over others' sweat-soaked work. Innovation happens when a community humbly comes together to discern how to be in a place in a way that blesses the lifeworld of a neighborhood.

Hopeprint is a wonderful example of innovation from the process of incarnation. Nicole was first introduced to Syracuse, New York's Northside several years ago, when the highest influx of resettled refugees into the neighborhood on record occurred. The families that she met and began to form friendships with became a daily beckoning to make their home her home as well. In the fall of 2010, Nicole and four others moved from the suburbs into the first Hopeprint Home on Lilac Street in the heart of the Northside. In this same season, Nicole and some initial partners officially started the organization Hopeprint. Dwelling in the neighborhood has brought a myriad of new friends, opportunities, and learning into her life. She often remarks that she has "learned more in the last three years than all of her schooling combined." Nicole firmly believes that all humanity has resting within them incredible potential, and wishes to see that potential realized in those around her—that they may "not just survive but thrive." She believes and lives out the paradigm that this is best done life on life, friend on friend. One is not teacher and another student, but rather we are all teachers and all students, growing together to be greater than the sum of our parts. Hopeprint innovated and called a faith community to step into the void.

As we innovate we ask:

- Does this really bless people?

- Is this rooted in our place?

- Are we pushing out other people by stepping in?

- How do we mourn with those who mourn?

- How do we form solidarity with those already here?

Improvisation

Improvisation is the process of devising a solution to a challenge by making do, despite an absence of resources that might be expected to produce a solution. Improvisation is the stage where we actualize our best ideas but understand that they may not be executed as we envisioned. We seek to be like a burning bush that declares God's presence through our embrace of those whose lives are seemingly different than our own. This is the body of Christ's mission. Our improvisation calls us into tangible solidarity with others. Listening to the ways the world has pummeled identities, we bend our lives into their pain, becoming a new people, a new embodied expression of Christ. Something new sprouts up in our improvisation. We learn to love in new challenging ways that surprise us. I experienced this surprise and scandal one night in my neighborhood. I had been living in my neighborhood for awhile, making friends with strangers that moseyed up and down my street. As an introvert this had been a hard practice for me, since I'd rather have my nose buried in a book somewhere in seclusion. Incrementally I'd been learning to introduce myself and ask questions related to people's stories, which opened me to the fun of hearing some wild tales. One night I saw a fellow sitting on a curb near my house and asked how he was doing. He looked at me with tearing eyes and said, "Not so good." I sat next to him as he slowly unraveled his complicated life, filled with regret, missed opportunities, abandoned friends, and addiction. He was a lonely brother. He asked if I could give him a ride to a different location so I did. As we drove together I could see him getting fidgety and sweaty. He then turned to me, grabbed my arm and demanded I give him money. I was angry and couldn't believe the betrayal. Suddenly I remembered these words from the Sermon on the Mount: "But to you who are listening I say: Love your enemies, do good to those who mistreat you. . . . If someone takes your coat, do not withhold your shirt from them. Give to everyone who asks you, and if anyone takes what belongs to you, do not demand it back" (Matt 5:38–42). Just to be clear, I did not have a surge of holiness rush through me, I was just being pestered and nagged by something I had read early in the week. I glared at him, trying to understand him one last time, and I said "here, take my whole bleepin' wallet," as my hands did something my mind hadn't approved yet. The black overstuffed wallet bounced into his hands and he looked at me with astonishment. We pulled up to the house I was dropping him off at; he got out and plunked down the unopened wallet in the passenger seat. I was a shaky mess, pondering if I should call the cops, but back then we didn't carry cell phones so going to a pay phone was a real inconvenience. I drove home in silence, pondering what had just happened and what God was saying to me. I was confronted with something, a private emotion: I don't love people. I don't hate them but I don't love them either. I know that's not cool to say as a church planter and community cultivator. I have sentimental love, maybe even theological love, but practical love comes and goes for me. I was wrestling with love in real-time practice. I wanted love on my terms without the disappointment of the up-close-and-personal space; yet there is no way to practice love without welcoming this irritation of incarnation. My friend came back around to my house a few weeks later as if the event had never occurred. We struck up an unlikely friendship and I helped him out in the best ways I could. We talked about everything and even a little bit about Jesus. I was in the midst of improvisation. My new friend wanted to be found out, not figured out. I was learning about the resistance within me; how unlove regularly rises to the top and floats on the surface of my heart. God is not interested in a professional compassion; he wants to take us through the labor process of birthing the real thing. Improvisation in my neighborhood with my kingdom community has brought me face to face with my own limits, impatience, stubbornness, and resentment. Trying to be present, really present in a particular place has ironically made me aware of what is present in me.

As we improvise we ask:

- Are our actions sustainable or are we looking for a quick return?
- What is being exposed in us as we improvise in this place?
- What resources could help us as we improvise?
- How can we draw others into partnership now that we are practicing?
- How do we build interdependence rather than dependence?

SUBMERGE TOOL

For most individuals, moving out of the fog of transience towards a new rooting in the relational labyrinth of a place can feel like wandering around in the dark. It takes a new schema to orient yourself in the scope of your place appropriately. Rooting in a place does not happen haphazardly, especially in our culture. It will take the building of new place-based scaffolding to reshape our choices to *be* somewhere purposefully. We need to form relational patterns in our daily, weekly, monthly, and yearly lives that shape us to be disciples of Jesus in our ordinary rhythms. We cannot think our way into rootedness. Our bodies and schedules need to seek a new ordering of going-about; this will cultivate new desires for our places. We are ritual beings who are fundamentally formed by what we *immerse* ourselves in. Caring and rooting in a place is not a novelty, it is a necessity for disciples. How do we be present with a sense of purpose that God's kingdom is among us, breaking in? We must begin to root below the buzz of marketing and self-promotion by submerging into a local context, getting tangible about how to foster connectivity with a place. Here is a basic schema for guiding each other into waking up our unique lifeworlds.

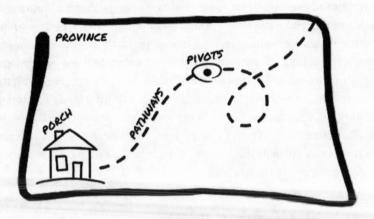

Porch—From Independence to Interdependence

"Which of the three became a neighbor? . . . The one who treated him kindly, so go and do likewise" (Luke 10:39–37).

I had a really interesting encounter a few years back when I visited an author who has written about issues of injustice in lower-income areas. As we walked up to his house I noticed that he passed his neighbors without an acknowledgment. I asked him later how he felt about the neighborhood and he said "It's nice." I admit I was probing but I asked him about his neighbors and he said, "They're cool, nobody bothers anyone." I found it ironic that an author writing about real people problems in real places didn't know or have much connection with his literal next-door neighbors. There is some subterfuge that occurs when we champion "loving like Jesus" but barely extend ourselves into the lives surrounding us. I'm convinced this is the first line of being a decent human. Before we think of changing the world we need to get to know our neighbors. "Neighbors" is not an abstract, over-spiritualized principle. Neighboring is the care we informally provide and receive from our neighbors. We are linked to our next-door neighbors and we can choose to leave static on the line or make a connection. Many have been raised to see neighbors as strangers we feel no obligation to overlap with. Typically our home is a realm of personal privacy insulated from the public world. The gospel makes it clear that inviting the "other" into our home is inviting the divine into our home—"Do not forget to show hospitality for by doing so some have shown hospitality to angels without knowing it" (Heb 13:2). In the place where I live there is so much pent-up dislike between neighbors that it's natural to safely tuck away. Jesus-followers can subvert this curse by practicing hospitality—moving beyond autonomy, fear, and misunderstanding into the uncharted space of conversation. Loving your neighbor is more than a lofty platitude.[7] *Do you know your neighbors?* Do you see your home first through the lens of protective security or sacred hospitality? I remember a time ten years ago being overly nervous about asking to borrow my neighbor's lawn mower. Why did something that was so normal become so unnatural for me? Time progressed and we began to build an interdependence that was life-giving for both of us. Many times I walked outside to see him working on something and I thought, "Should I walk over to help him? It could eat up my day." These concerns are real but they act as boundaries that impede the movement of trust in one another, paralyzing us and perpetuating distance.[8] There is something equalizing about sharing food. We have a family in our community that does an inspiring job of creating connector points using food. Smash the sentiment of loving neighbors through the sharing of food. The *porch* is symbolic of your first place of being in a place.

- Are we open to using our home for hospitality with neighbors?
- Am I open to sharing with my neighbors?
- Do I know my neighbors' names?
- Have I offered to help them, shovel their driveway, and babysit their kids?
- Do I use holidays to create connector points: birthdays, Christmas, Hanukkah, etc.?

7. Pathack and Runyan, *The Art of Neighboring*, 45–47.

8. Walljasper, *The Great Neighborhood Book*, 55–58.

Pathways—From Unconscious Busyness to Conscious Habitation

" Walking along the street, Jesus saw a man blind and stopped to attend to him" (John 9:1).

In downtown New York City a heroic man was stabbed while attempting to save a Queens woman from a knife-wielding attacker. As surveillance video revealed, he lay dying in a pool of blood for more than an hour as nearly twenty-five people indifferently strolled past him.[9] Most of the passers-by moved hurriedly by without much of a pause. Not until some thirty minutes after the victim collapsed did firefighters finally arrive and discover the man had died. The indifference of the pedestrians echoed the infamous 1964 murder of Kitty Genovese in Kew Gardens, Queens, where the same thing happened. Did people ignore the crime scene or were they too busy to notice? I think they were too busy to notice. Certainly this is an exaggerated example but often we are slaves to unconscious traveling, withdrawing into minimal interactions. We are often dragged around by busyness so much that we do not see, acknowledge, or engage with people along our path. We've become an antisocial people, and the people of God must create contours of resistance to this modern evolution. *Pathways* are the routes we take every day. The pathways we take shape our understanding of the city. We must gain a better environmental presence or we will become isolated from the place that we are a part of, making people along our routes nameless and faceless. This requires a shift. How do we move to astute listening along our pathway? Something simple that I seek to practice often is walking my dog and greeting passersby and asking questions of curiosity. On my walk I always pass a bus stop and stop to talk to a guy named Reggie. Sure, I miss my commitment to walk the dog once in awhile but I'm habitual enough that Reggie has become a human to me and I've become human to him. A reciprocal human process is sprouting. *Are we looking, do we have eyes to see?* A young woman in our community has been working this into her life and was walking down the sidewalk. She looked across the street and saw a boy shooting some baskets at his rusty basketball hoop. She felt a compulsion to walk over and ask to shoot some hoops with him. His face lit up and they struck up a friendship. This little boy introduced her to his family. They were refugees from the Congo. They spoke little English but they bonded immediately with my friend. This young woman was overwhelmed with the nest of needs she walked into.

9. Livingston, "Stabbed Hero Dies."

They shared a need for school supplies, so she invited another member in our community to join her in helping. Together they've begun a rich relationship with this family simply because this woman in our community opened her eyes along her *pathway*.

- What routes do we want to take to engage with our neighborhood?
- Do we walk? Do we drive?
- Are there people along our pathways we've never noticed?
- Are we open to stopping along the path?
- Are we consistent in our pathways?

Pivots—From Consuming Perks to Beholding People

"Jesus passed through Samaria . . . and Jacob's well was still there. Jesus, worn out by the trip, sat down at the well. It was noon. A woman, a Samaritan, came to draw water. Jesus said, 'Could I have a drink of water?'" (John 4:4–8).

Mister Rogers is a bit of a hero of mine. His half-hour television show ran from 1966 to 2001. Mr. Rogers was an easygoing fellow who thoroughly engaged and enjoyed his neighborhood. Every show was filled with his neighborhood visits popping in on King Friday, X the Owl, Lady Elaine, Harriet Elizabeth Cow, and Henrietta Pussycat. Mr. Rogers is an inspiration to us. Maybe some of it is a bit hokey and dated but being a face in the place is essential to rooting in a place. A pivot is a spot where different sorts of people mingle, where relational intersections occur. When you pivot, there are people within arm's reach. There is a coffee shop I frequent that would be easy to hide out in as I sip on my espresso. Instead, over the years I've had to learn to make introductions, ask questions, always acknowledge, engage, and remember names. There's a barista who recently asked, "Are you counselor or something?" It was an interesting observation and I replied, "Not really, I just like to know who people are." His response is branded on my mind: "Well, no one likes to do that anymore, do they?" My hipster espresso artist may be right. Rootedness begins when these points of contact are nurtured. Can you imagine if beholding the people at our pivot points became Christianity 101 for disciples? There would be seedlings of life being cultivated in subterranean ways all over the place without one dollar spent to launch a big church program. A convergence of people from different tribes' park in that coffee shop. Recently a group of people sitting in a circle were knitting, drinking coffee, and talking about politics. I couldn't help but stick my head into find out about this quirky mix. They welcomed me in and I made some new friends. Our pivots are vital places where the kingdom of God leaks into our day. Become intentional about them. Gain eyes of faith for holy interruptions and sustainable habits. The biggest temptation we face is to overlook people, seeing them as commodities to serve our needs, not people that matter to God.

- Are you a regular?

- Have you made introductions?

- What communities collide at your pivot points?

- Where are your regular pivots (the YMCA, McD's, the bus stop, the park, the pub, etc.)?

Province—From Indifference to Responsibility

"Leaving Nazareth he went and lived in Capernaum" (Matt 4:13).

I remember the feelings like it was yesterday. I was panic stricken, whimpering and unable to find any light. The world was closing in on me. I was ten years old and playing laser tag in a huge dark maze. At one point I had gotten confused and all the other kids were on the opposite side of the maze and now it was silent and I could not see. I had no idea where I was in the maze; everything looked and felt the same. Disorientation is what I experienced. Disorientation is when our equilibrium of where we are is distorted or nonexistent. Many people have disorientation when it comes to where they live, as they are unknowing of the emotional and physical needs, opportunities, and social movements in their place.[10] Finding orientation in a broader physical environment is essential for the formation of identity and being the expression of Jesus in our place. *Province* as a British term is used to describe a *sphere of life* in a section of a city or suburb. A province is a smaller area within a larger area that contains an infrastructure of concentrated culture, business, and residence. Our ability to emotionally attach and resonate with a place has a scope and size. A province is a manageable section of our city that we can feel some sense of responsibility to. Seeing our place with generic eyes is a hindrance to the missional impulse. When

10. Beatley, *Native to Nowhere*, 80–82.

we do not understand the self within a place it becomes easy to disconnect our actions from the welfare of our place. How we live, how others live, should matter to us. As we root in our province the aches of this place become our aches. The authors of *The New Parish* say it well: "The parish is the places where a local church identifies by a large enough space to live life together and a small enough space to be known as characters within."[11] I am using the word *province* in very much the same way. Wherever we live we must seek to understand our province, embracing our human-scaled environment. The more we understand about the character of our province the more importance it will take on in our lives. As we strengthen our emotional bonds to a bite-size portion of our city/town we form a location devotion.[12] We move from a me to we. Additionally, in our exploration of being in a place we begin to look for others who are taking responsibility for this province. I remember sitting in the hotel ballroom turned into a church as the pastor rallied a gathering of people around the mantra "save the city because no one else will." Like vultures people swarmed in excitement to this vision for being the church where there were no churches. *Yet is this true? Is this healthy?* We have a natural tendency to be myopic when we set out do something significant in a place. We gain energy by spinning a narrative that "no one else is doing what I'm doing." In my section of the city there are brothers and sisters of every ethnicity who have been faithfully working for renewal in this place. We have differing theologies and personalities but it would be quite arrogant for me to claim sole hero status in my place. Our territorialism is destructive to the flourishing of the kingdom of God. The first-century disciples were very much like us. "Master, we saw someone driving out demons in your name and we tried to stop him, because he is not one of us." Jesus said, "Do not stop him, for whoever is not against you is for you." (Mark 9:38–39.)The disciples had a strong "us versus them" mentality even though they knew what it felt like to be outsiders in the empire. We must fight this impulse to claim a hero complex. God is doing something significant in your province: spread out your arms to lay hold of it.

- What observations have we made about our province?

- How do we fuel a love for this place?

- What is the beauty in our place?

11. Sparks, Soerens, and Friesen, *The New Parish*, 76–77.
12. Manzo and Deveine-Wright, "Beyond House and Haven," 47.

- What is the brokenness in our place?
- How do we make the pains of this place our pains?

10

Rooting in Community

I'M A TOTAL SCI-FI fanatic. I especially get giddy about the post-apocalyptic genre of movies and books. Sometimes nothing gets me more jazzed up than nibbling on a bag of Sour Patch Kids and digging into a fresh dystopian cinema experience. I'm fascinated with the concept of how humanity survives when the structures previously depended upon are no longer dependable. When everything collapses the basic structure of humanity moves to the forefront: *community*. One of my favorite movies last year was the beautifully filmed movie *Oblivion*. In the year 2077, Jack Harper is a technician living in a tower high above the clouds. In a war that Jack can't remember because his memory has been erased for security reasons, humans were forced to use nuclear weapons to destroy aliens who wanted to take over the planet. In the end humans won the war, but lost the earth by turning most of it into a radioactive wasteland. Jack's job is to journey to the surface during the day to repair drones that extract the earth's remaining resources. One day Jack goes to work and is instructed by his superior to investigate a beacon signal on the planet. When Jack arrives he finds nothing unusual on the desolate planet earth, so he decides to take a nap on the grass. When he awakens he sees objects in the distance crashing down from the sky. He goes and finds real humans in sleep pods scattered about the wreckage. A woman escapes from a pod and knocks Jack unconscious. He awakens to find himself captured in a cave and tied to a chair. A man reveals himself to be part of the Human Resistance. He tells Jack that the drones are actually programmed to kill any humans remaining on earth.

The leader of the resistance, Beech, tells Jack that a community of people have been hiding out in caves, surviving and gearing up to reclaim the planet. Jack is in disbelief until he meets the people gathering in the caves. This experience brings into question everything he believed about the war.

In some ways this is how I lean into "being the church." *How can the Western body of Christ survive the impending collapse of Christendom? How will the church survive the future?* The increasing irrelevance of the Christian industrial complex propping up our Christian celebrities and offering Christian alternatives to everything might be a sobering blessing in disguise. Rather than going back to the boardroom to come up with more ingenious ways to be relevant, we should pick through the mound of our seeming progress to recover the neglected gem of *community*.

THE RAW MATERIAL

To be radically rooted we must unpack the raw material of the early church's social existence together. The Acts 2 Pentecost event was the start of the Jesus movement but it did not sustain itself in that fashion. Those early chapters *do not* give us a correct view of the way the early church maintained and thrived. We get a descriptive window into the beginning of things, not a prescription for how it was sustained. The New Testament is not a record of big explosive event after big explosive event. After the powerful kingdom interruption of Pentecost the church became a movement, a seedling posture, scattering into small household clusters.[1] It is saturated with small, oppressed, faithful spiritual families trying to survive under an empire. The church at Jerusalem distributed itself into micro assemblies in far-flung parts of Judea. These community pods are what the New Testament calls *oikos,* a Greek term typically translated "house" or "household."[2] It refers to the basic building block of society, its close network of relationships. The average membership of a New Testament church was around twenty to forty, like the one that met in Troas (Acts 20:9) These communities gathered in different pockets throughout a city, becoming "the body of Christ" in that place. The explosive quality of the gospel of Jesus was that Jews and Gentiles, women and men, slaves and free were being knit together to declare something with profound social implications. In the mind of a first-century Hebrew, Gentiles were created as kindling for the fires of

1. Banks, *Paul's Idea of Community,* 57–58.
2. Gehring, *House Church and Mission,* 44–46.

hell and Gentiles regarded Jews to be subhuman. A new species was being created that was blowing the circuitry of every person living in century one. It shook the Roman Empire to its very foundations.[3] Former enemies were now sharing a meal, orbiting around the bread and wine of Jesus the Messiah. The conduit of community was not a quaint 1960s vibe—it was a marker that the kingdom of God was making trouble in the Mediterranean. It was rumbling from below, forming new spiritual clusters. In the imagination of first-century Judaism, the Temple existed as the dwelling of Israel's God with daily and yearly sacrifices through which fellowship with this God would be assured. A new Temple was being constructed but it didn't look like impressive brick and mortar; rather the Temple morphed into what might seem like an underdog situation, a relational network of communities. This was the space of God's new dwelling pulling previously polarized people together.

THE COMMUNITY ORGANIZER

These scattered Christian communities expressed their newfound unity not by fashioning a corporate organization that could rival their secular competitors; instead their newfound unity was expressed in the simplicity yet complexity of mutual love in community. Very little machinery was in place to veil this love for which the communities labored. This love was left naked and exposed for all to see. Community illuminated the centrality of love. It left its imprint on every facet of social existence. Without the axiom of love the early church's bonds would fizzle into fragments. The enormity of this cannot be underestimated. They did not have the shiny trussing of well-rehearsed worship bands, magnetic preachers, and packaged Bible study material to buffer their church life. There was little to hide behind. This is what is jarring and jolting about what transpired: they had to love one another to stay together. This is why the Apostle Paul sounded like a community organizer.[4] The images we have of Paul can't help but be constructed in our imaginations in terms of our modern jobs, careers, and ministry roles. So we fashion Paul into an evangelist in the modern sense, a powerful orator and a professional theologian. These images shape how we read his letters and regard his central concerns. Still, Paul's primary passion was that churches eagerly mature as unified communities of self-sacrificial love. The

3. Viola, *Reimagining Church*, 67–68.
4. Gombis, "The Apostle Paul."

image of a community organizer is a person walking through neighbor-hoods, sleeves rolled up, getting to know people, trying to understand local problems, and working to resolve conflicts and solve problems.[5] Paul is a diagnostician with the mechanics of community when he says in his Epistle, "Put on compassion, kindness, lowliness, meekness and patience, bearing with one another, forgiving one another and above all this put on love, which binds you together in perfect harmony" (Col 3:12–14). Love that forged harmony was not a saccharine idea; it was a foundational value to kingdom community life. He also tells the household church in Thessa-lonica "to increase and abound in love for one another" (1 Thess 3:2) and tells the Galatian church that a chief fruit of the spirit is love (Gal 5:22). Love moves past sentiment and takes the shape of concrete acts with each other. The truth of love cannot be communicated except as it is embodied in a community. The gospel of Jesus wired people to share life together and that was a social mushroom cloud on the horizon of the first-century world.

THE MOLECULE OF LOVE

A new field, called interpersonal neurobiology, draws its vigor from one of the great discoveries of our era: the brain is constantly rewiring itself. In the end, what we pay the most attention to literally rewires our brains. The most formative and dramatic rewiring occurs based on the quality of our relational bonds that foster or fail us. As imaging studies by the neu-roscientist Naomi Eisenberger show, for better or for worse we are social beings.[6] These neurons of relating *fire together* based on how much care

5. Ibid.
6. Ackerman, "Brain on Love."

we *give* and *receive* from a social structure to which we're attached. If there is minimal *giving* and *receiving* then our brains change. Infants register an indelible sense of "feeling felt" or being "left alone" and it changes them, but we're discovering the *changing* is still ongoing in adulthood. Reciprocity of relationship refashions our inner architecture. Loving relationships alter the brain the most significantly. As the brain registers loving relationships it begins to extend its idea of self to include others. Instead of the slender pronoun "I," a plural self emerges that begins to borrow some of the others' assets and strengths. The brain rewires for a new identity that is "who we are." This is just some of the social science behind what was occurring in the consciousness of the New Testament churches. In many ways the early Jesus communities can be compared to a molecule. A molecule consists of atoms that are held together by an unbreakable bond. Atoms no longer find their identity in the power of their individuality but in the power of their interdependence. Individualism offers the illusion that our choices, beliefs, and application of those beliefs happen best in a vacuum of our own will and wants. This is an illusion because for better or worse we live our beliefs *together*. This is where we get the word *religion*, which means to tie, to bind.[7] Many don't want to be bound, but we are. We're caught up in a dynamic, complicated web of beliefs that will bind us to someone, somewhere. I'd rather break the delusion that I live on an island and be intentional about those bonds and the quality of that interdependence.

Community was not an invention whipped up by God for the purpose of getting the early Jesus movement rolling. The pulse of vital interdependence found in the early church has its origins in the DNA of the Trinity. Community is at the center of the Godhead. Before there was ever the mission of designing the Genesis world, there was God three-in-one. God is neither lonely nor alone, for from the beginning, the Father, Son, and Holy Spirit have been in an unending waltz of mutual love with one another, and they invite us into their community so that we might learn what it means to be a community.[8] When it comes to creating humanity God does not simply speak a word of command but engages in conversation amongst the Trinity[9]—"let *us* make mankind in our image" (Gen 1:26). This is communal, not individualistic. Our personhood in relation to God is defined in relational terms. We are relational beings who cannot understand the na-

7. Sharlett, *Radiant Truths,* 77–81.

8. Woodward, *Creating a Missional Culture,* 89–90.

9. White Jr., "The Source of Community."

ture of God and ourselves outside community. In the narrative of Scripture we see brightly that God is a social rather than a solitary being.

Community orbits around love but love is faced with a tug-of-war over definitions; the yanking back and forth is between the metaphors of friendship or family. In the New Testament, family is the preeminent metaphor used for explaining community.[10] Many have experienced destructive families, certainly making that metaphor rest uneasily. But the family metaphor is not one of a modern nuclear family. It is one of a redeemed community. Jesus chose the word *family* as the defining metaphor for describing the disciple community he gathered. Family required the highest work of faithfulness, relational identification with each other, and commitment past the point of conflict. Consumerism promises to alleviate inconvenience but community promises to mature us if we stay faithful during inconvenience. Jesus wove this into the quilt of the gospel very early on. The Apostle Paul sees great implications for envisioning ourselves as family members: "work for the good of all but especially for those in our family of faith" (Gal 6:10) and "for you are no longer strangers and sojourners but members of the family of God" (Eph 2:18). In my work in cultivating communities I've met many well meaning people who seek community looking for friendship, *not* family, but friendship is extremely fickle and selective. Friendship seeks a certain compatibility that cannot often be verbalized. Honestly, we like to bond with people with whom we have chemistry. Here's one embarrassing example of how fickle friendship can be: a few years back I was getting to know a few guys I was playing basketball with. We'd go out after the game and get a few drinks. There was one fellow who loved the same football team I did, so we naturally had a ton to talk about. After basketball one night someone pointed out that the Ultimate Fighting Championship (UFC) was on the TV overhead. Well, my burgeoning new friend's adrenal glands shot to eleven. He loved UFC and almost lost his voice screaming about about how amazing it was and how much he watched it. I almost dry heaved. I loathe UFC for many reasons and I had a hard time chilling with him after that. Maybe that's a bit petty, but we all do this to varying degrees. We do choose our bonds based on idiosyncratic compatibilities. Friendship seeks affinity and affinity is about *likeness*. Affinity is a harmless and wonderful experience in friendship but *likeness* can play a destructive role in our ability to love. Affinity is the major way we organize ourselves in the modern world. This is the ancient Greek concept of *philia* love, which

---

10. Hellerman, *When Church Was Family*, 35–37.

is often translated as friendship. Aristotle said that "philia is for pleasure, based on pure delight in the company of other people. People who drink together may have such friendships but they also may part when they find each other uninteresting."[11] This kind of love demands to be loved on "my terms." Friendship or *philia* love is not a strong enough glue to hold people together in community; at the first offense the glue of *philia* breaks down. The sad separating of the church into "like" groups and programs doesn't cultivate New Testament community. When we split out into moms with toddlers, hipsters with tattoos, people who watch Fox News, people who watch Colbert for their news, the urban poor, men who like to hunt, or middle-aged folks with good jobs, we don't look like the people of God. We're only mimicking our consumeristic, individualistic counterparts. This affinity-based relational quarantining has become extremely evident along the lines of political preferences.

Based on the largest study of US political attitudes ever undertaken by the Pew Research Center, a social dividing is aggressively ordering us into "political siloing"—the tendency to interact mostly with like-minded people. Voters (50 percent) say that it's "important to live in a place where most people share my political views." Similarly, 63 percent of staunch conservatives say most of their friends share their world view, while 49 percent of liberals say the same.[12] Partisan animosity has increased substantially. We are being shaped by the political character of our day and it is deeply distorting our ability to live into real-time community. The best way to punch a hole in the ideological echo chamber is faithfulness to an on-the-ground community. There is a gravitational pull to align myself *with* a camp and *against* a camp. It takes intentional countercultural effort to form a quality of life together not using the weak mortar of *philia*. If we are honest, what we dislike the most is being in community with those we dislike the most. We may certainly find the joy of friendship in community but friendship is not the rallying point of community. When the Apostle Paul speaks of the brand of love in community he does not use the Greek *philia* but the word *agape* in reference to familial love. We hear *agape* often referenced in marriage ceremonies but very little within the micro-space of Christian community. *Agape* is the bonding agent in community. It is a love that gives itself to others irrespective of the reaction it receives. It is not a limited love seeking to be part of the rank and file of likeness.

11. Aristotle, *Nicomachean Ethics*, 110–12.

12. Holland, "Pew Research Study."

I know many in the pursuit of the project of community have been wounded and left with scars. Poisonous relationships can plunder the bank of our souls. We must mourn these realities and name wrongs, yet we cannot hide from one another. That which protects us from pain also protects us from love. We might plan to always have an umbrella to protect us from the rain but we'll get caught without it eventually. The pain of relating will soak us; there's no way to avoid it. Our hurts must press us to reach deeper into the work of redemptive community. I've learned that in weaving together community there is always a needle that could potentially poke. This why we can appreciate the work of community formation in the first-century church all the more. Their struggle to root together in the midst of offenses, fragmentation, arguing, gossip, and theological disagreement is very much our struggle. The consistent work of cultivating healthy communities has been compared to peeling an onion.[13] I love onions and throw them in almost any dish my wife and I are cooking. But despite my love for onions, when I begin to peel back its layers, tears well up in my eyes. As we persevere in rooting in community we peel back layers of ourselves and our relationships, which brings a certain amount of travail and even tears. This travail is the work of love. We cannot learn to love without this pain. Love is school, but the tuition is high and the homework can be painful.[14] When Christian communities attempt to construct community around friendship, they craft with anemic materials that cannot survive the disruption of offenses; rather community must look to form *fidelity* rather than *affinity*. Community is where we can experience the incredible privilege of being ourselves in the presence of love. Learning to love people we wouldn't naturally like is an essential point of becoming a disciple of Jesus. Henri Nouwen has said, "Community is the fruit of our capacity to make the interests of others more important than our own."[15] What Paul has in mind as a community organizer is a love that can handle the weight of suffering, differences, and time.

BULWARKED SELF

A reorientation around community might make us squirm, since our own happiness and satisfaction typically takes precedence over group identity.

13. Janzen, *The Intentional Christian Community*, 120–25.

14. Ackerman, "Brain on Love."

15. Nouwen, *In the Name of Jesus*, 52–53.

We see ourselves as individuals first and foremost, and bounce among groups as they help us inch closer to our individual goals.[16] We're conditioned to interface with communities by asking what they can do for us rather than the other way around; this feels so normal and natural for us. We think we can develop a healthy self apart from community. I confess that in my twenties I did not critique this impulse in myself. I'm not sure I was even aware how utilitarian I was in my approach to community. I've learned that sacrifice is always required in order to stay put with people because personal ambitions will always interrupt fidelity. Everyone says they want community. However, because it takes commitment we find ways to move on. This squirm and suspicion around community is convoluted by our emotional understandings of freedom. *What is freedom?* Freedom defined in the West is freedom of choice, freedom *from*. Our imaginations of freedom are shaped by the right to be my own person. Never do I think that community should obliterate individual uniqueness: this would be a violent community, not redeemed community. Freedom, however, has snowballed into an icon standing for separation from most anything we deem unworthy of our time or from obligations to people we find uninteresting. Freedom in the New Testament was a mechanism not *from* people but *for* people. Freedom moved from a self-orientation to an others-centered orientation, reflected in Jesus high priestly prayer: "I have given them the glory which you have given me, so that they may be one as we are one, I in them and you in me, that they may be completely one, so that the world may know that you sent me, and that you loved them just as you loved me" (John 17:22). This prayer is not simply aiming for us to get along with plastic niceties, it is pushing against every social milieu seeking to parcel us out into separate spaces. Our associations and relationships are narrower and narrower. Despite having connections everywhere we have bulwarked our beings. Our over-connectedness with affinity pipelines like Twitter, Facebook, blogs, and the like has created detached relating. Our connections are made anemic as they are associated with Facebook verbs like "friending" and "unfriending." We are more unsure of ourselves than ever and this is directly related to the way individualism has bulwarked us.[17] We've hemmed ourselves in with so much that we are protected from the rub of intimacy. We are self-sufficient, able to Google our question rather than asking someone for help in community. Or we change our minds on

16. Arpin-Ricci, *The Cost of Community*, 47–48.

17. Stassen, *A Thicker Jesus*, 123–25.

an issue after reading a book, never working it out in conversation in community. Individualism soaks our bones so much that inviting a community into our decisions creates more panic than peace. Community can be a terribly frustrating place for one who wants to go it alone and decide alone. There is a widespread intoxication in our day that human beings flourish to the degree they are free to satisfy their own personal desires.[18] In our enlightened arrogance we think we are more open-minded but we are more closed off than we've ever been. The bulwarked self amasses a fortress of information, technology, platforms,and status to advance one's own cause without actually settling and submitting to others.

For those of us born and bred in the good old U-S-of-A, we approach things with a hyper-individualistic orientation. We are weaned on the idea of autonomy when it comes to our ability to climb the spiritual ladder. We naturally envision ourselves "taking on" or "collapsing under" whatever spiritual challenged is laid out before us. This is not the imagination of the New Testament family. Without a strong rootedness in community a shadow of sadness is the result, because intimacy with others seems more and more like a fairy tale. The world peddles its solutions for a better life while installing more buffers on the hard drive of our identities. There is a sense of malaise, emptiness, and cynicism that settles in our isolation, which creates disenchantment with the world. Our bodies are not being shaped for the reception of community. This isolation causes dehumanization in our ability to feel deep concern for others who are unlike us. It is in close quarters in community that we learn how to grow up into empathy, listening, compassion, slowness to speak, constancy, and a host of other character traits. In the book *The Virtue of Selfishness*, Ayn Rand cautions people to put self before others, seeing group commitment as a threat to autonomy.[19] This might sound extreme but the venomous force of it has crept into the church and we unknowingly reinforce it with the way we organize for being the church. There is a difference between church as an incorporated entity and church as a community of people. Many churches have become little more than gatherings of isolated individuals.

18. Reno, *Genesis*, 94–95.
19. Rand, *The Virtue of Selfishness*, 130–31.

PEEP CULTURE

Peep culture provides us with a semblance of community while protecting ourselves from the real thing. In Hal Nidzviecki's eerie book *The Peep Diaries*, he states. "Peep culture is reality TV, Twitter, Instagram and Facebook. It's blogs, chat rooms, amateur porn sites, viral digital movies of a fat kid pretending to be a Jedi Knight, cell phone photos—posted online—and citizen surveillance videos. Peep is the backbone of Web 2.0 . . . and it's everywhere, all day, all the time."[20] We can carry on vicarious feelings of intimacy through watching and commenting. Our neurons are being fused to relate through buffers. Social media is making us antisocial. Peep culture cajoles us into fostering a persona-product that bolsters our ideal identity online while undermining our crumbling sense of community. A confessional, a memoir online has become the preferred avenue for authenticity, making the real thing even more frightening and not worth the risk. This was why I was fascinated by the elements of the Manti Te'o drama in January 2013. Manti Te'o, a college football player, was hoaxed when his online girlfriend faked her death. Te'o said that his girlfriend, Stanford University student Lennay Kekua, had died after a car accident. Te'o explained that he kept it from most people because he thought he would be seen as "crazy" for having a serious relationship with a woman he had never met. An acquaintance of Te'o's confessed to orchestrating a hoax that lured Te'o into an online relationship with a nonexistent woman. This young man fell in love with an avatar. *How did a young man build a strong emotional attachment with someone that was not physically in his life? How did he develop a perceived relationship with someone who was not actively present?* Something about this story symbolizes a cultural shift in how we've begun to quantify community. The Manti Te'o experience is indicative of the story we find ourselves in. He was able to assemble some of the contents of a relationship without having an actual tethered relationship. To him the relationship was real, which is the point. To Manti Te'o the relationship was meeting his emotional needs. It is possible to put together the semblance of community—"a little of this and a little of that"—and end up with a self-selected substitute community.[21] Relationships operating this way inevitably turn people into pieces that can be swapped out and replaced. We live in a time with many connections, but very few bonds.

20. Neidzviecki, *The Peep Diaries,* 46–48.
21. Pohl, *Living Into Community,* 25–27.

ROOTED IDENTITY

Stanley Hauerwas has said, "The role of the prophet has been given to an entire community."[22] The community stands as a protest against the tyranny of individualism pointing to the renewed world under the reign of King Jesus. Community is an anarchist move in some ways as it shifts power from institutions to ordinary clustered people. To be rooted in community is to understand it is "not good for us to be alone." We are floating disembodied spirits when we are not tethered to an embodied spiritual family in a physical place. The inertia of the world is splintering our identities away and outward from a grounded people and we must rebel. The church does not need to compete with the technologies of constant stimulation when the future will be marked by the secure community we create. Radical rootedness flips the trajectory of casual connections and plummets into vital connections. More than attending an event or volunteering at a worship service we need to recalibrate ourselves with others.

What does it mean to be me with others?

What does it mean to be a contributor in community?

We are told that to form identity is to differentiate ourselves from others, clarifying who we are over and against others. Certainly we are all unique, with special interests, quirky personalities, and personal stories. Still this is not the hot center of identity formation. The fierce journey of differentiation to be an individual has ironically perpetuated more identity crisis than identity security. Jesus understood himself not as a solo astronaut blazing through the world on his own, proving his awesomeness. Jesus' self-understanding was rooted in the Trinity and love that flows downward from that fullness.

22. Hauerwas, *Matthew*, 71.

11

Practicing Community

ANY *WALKING DEAD* FANS out there? I find the show fascinating from a sociological perspective, besides the epic nature of the plot with the world overrun by zombies. What is center stage is the fragility of human community. As the group of survivors are on a mission to secure a base camp what is most unsafe and unstable is not necessarily the zombies, it is actual people. One of our elders at our church recently stated that *The Walking Dead* is an illustration of how community affects mission. Dale, one of the older and wiser characters, says, "It's not the walkers out there that will kill us; it's what's going on in here." It is their slowly self-destructing relationships that erode the survivors' ability to stay focused on the mission at hand.

Nothing has humbled my seeming leadership intelligence more over the years than living into and cultivating healthy community. Every community includes a zoo of unspoken ideals and ideas of community. The Apostle Paul counsels the church in Thessalonica, "Regarding your life together, get along with each other. Take this seriously, love one another!" (1 Thess 3:9). One of our foremost responsibilities is to assess, identify, stimulate, and disciple healthy habits within community. The work of community if neglected will always sabotage mission, so let's get particular.

GETTING PARTICULAR

The challenge in community formation is moving from idealism to realism. Idealism is the epistemological doctrine that mental ideas are the most fundamental reality. Essentially, it is any philosophy which argues that the only thing actually knowable is in our consciousness. René Descartes was one of the first to claim that all we really know is what is in our own consciousnesses, and that the whole external world is merely an idea or picture in our minds. Therefore, he claimed, it is possible to doubt the reality of the external world as consisting of real objects, and "I think, therefore I am" is the only assertion that cannot be doubted. Idealism in its many forms infects our ability to accept reality, work within reality, and find contentment within reality. Idealism is in direct contrast to realism, which holds that the truest things are what are physically before us and can be touched with our hands. Idealism has infiltrated most of society and encourages us to exalt our preferred dreams as authority over the raw relational material before us. Idealism perpetuates self-love for our own ideas and creates delusion that we actually live up to our own ideas. Idealism compels us into an ever-ready state of criticism, measuring everything against our perceived perfect picture of how things should be. Idealism causes us to love an ideal community that reflects ourselves rather than sacrificial love for a real enfleshed community. Our ideal relational life in community can become an idol not grounded in the brokenness of real people with real problems. Idealism poisons us regarding the realities of messy practice. We must move into the real and get particular in our emotional and relational scaffolding, to assemble a sustainable life together that will always need a heavy dose of grace as our WD-40.

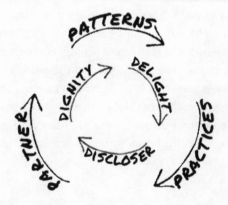

AVAILABILITY AND VULNERABILITY

Availability and vulnerability are the fabric of community because we really never get away from them. The need for availability and vulnerability is always with us, like the ground beneath our feet. We may stroll and not blatantly point out that the ground is there beneath our feet: "Hey, look everyone, there is pavement holding me up." The moment an earthquake breaks the ground beneath our feet away we will notice with intensity that we cannot stand up straight without it. Availability and vulnerability comprise the basic ground floor of community that help us stand up and find our center of gravity in the world. For too long the church has attempted to function without them, creating *uprooted* and *unstable* humans. We must come out of the fog of individualism and into the light of community. In this chapter we'll attempt to move past the idealism of community and into real reorientation.

AVAILABILITY

Availability is the first social construct we encounter together. We cannot move towards the inner life of vulnerability in community without a sturdy availability to each other. A history of availability will build a bridge to vulnerability, as availability closes the gulf between people.

We do need to *choose* to be together. We are so acculturated toward individualism that we need to choose against all our inner conditioning. A choice to be available is a choice to live into greater meaning, a choice of responsibility. The consumer toxins still in our bloodstream will whisper "what's in it for me?" but entitlement erodes community.[1] Our Western individualism teaches us that we can have community without being encumbered. Availability is the pathway between our individual existence and our collective experience.

Availability and Patterns

A pattern is a template, a discernible regularity in the world that is designed by humans. The elements of a pattern are repeatable in a dependable manner. Patterns are integral, seeding change in our character and competencies. In forming community we must seek to find a pattern that works but stretches

1. McKnight and Block, *Abundant Community,* 45–47.

us. Lesslie Newbigin has said, "We are shaped by what we attend to."[2] We must refresh what will conform us into a love-filled, grounded people, for the good of the world and the glory of God. I'm a minimalist, believing that the power is in the *essentials* not the *luxuries*. From that perspective I ask "what are those essential patterns we must cultivate that foster a vibrant available life together in the world?" We are human so our joy, energy, and emotional maturity towards living *as the church* ebbs and flows, which makes it paramount to mutually commit to foundational patterns. Community patterns are not about control but constancy, making space for each other to depend on each other. A good parallel is that my ten-year-old son and I have a regular date to go out for breakfast on Saturday mornings. No matter how crazy the week is we try to meet for a greasy spoon breakfast to laugh and talk about superheroes. This not only helps me stay faithful to being with my son, but from my son's vantage point he has something dependable to lean on. Patterns of availability in community function the same way, allowing us to depend on each other. There is an incremental revival that happens in our communal consistency. Make new commitments to be available through regularly shared meals, babysitting each other's kids, working on each other's house projects, making mutual purchases of tools to share, shopping together, reading together, playing together, enjoying holidays together, cooking together, and even moving closer to one another. This inhabiting ethos creates fresh possibilities. This takes time, time, time to massage into our DNA. Within our patterns we foster a common life together. Sit down and talk about the patterns of availability you want reflected in your day, your week, your month, your year. Communities must seek pattern specificity that is malleable with grace. We often fear patterns because they hem us in and challenge our haphazardness. There is grace for each other in our forgetfulness and failures. Still we must seek to submit to a pattern of availability if we desire a generous, robust life together.

2. Newbigin, *The Open Secret*, 96–97.

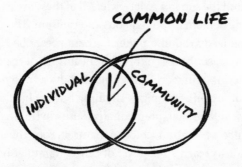

Let spontaneity emerge from your stable patterns with each other. The "pop-in" has become a no-no in our culture. Living in a primarily African American neighborhood I've been blessed to observe the "pop-in," stopping by unannounced, swinging by the porch just to check in. This has been a beautiful gift we are attempting to work out in our church communities: to be available to each other on a whim. Recently my wife and I were away and our lawn got wildly overgrown. Someone in our community spontaneously mowed it for us, so when we pulled in after our long drive I was greeted by their gift to us. More than just relieving me of work it communicated value and love to me. When you go to the farmers market pick up a dozen extra eggs to spontaneously drop off to a neighbor. When you're going out for a dinner, call to see if someone might drop everything and meet you there. Break someone's stressful day by surprising them with soup. I used to think spontaneity was just a nicety; I now have experienced it as deeply meaningful for communicating availability to each other. Jesus' statement about "let the little children come to me" (Matt 19:14) was certainly a statement on the worth of children but it was also a statement on the beauty of inconvenience. Children invade and burst through our schedules. This is the way Jesus treats all of humanity. He does not worship his plan of action before presence with people. Let your life be interrupted. Community also involves a willingness to be available to the interruption of pain, crisis, and trauma. Listen for these, look for these. Work towards patterns and in your rhythm look for the interruptions.

The Frequency: What Is the Pattern of Our Coming Together?

All of life is built upon patterns. In the natural world bees form their honeycombs methodically, robins put together their nests piece by piece, and planets loop around the sun in a strict cycle. All of these are wild expressions in nature, yet none of them is spontaneous and random. They are exuberant but they are organized around a pattern. These prescribed patterns form the platform for robust displays of brilliant beauty. Patterns on the surface can seem constricting, stiffly organic expression. It's a funny thing, organic farming is hip but organic farming is anything but haphazard. Ask any organic farmer how intentional, premeditated, and rhythmic their toiling is in order to produce a bountiful, colorful, natural crop. The goal in finding a frequency is not to reach some level of self-congratulation but rather a pattern that shapes something beautiful in our midst. If you're gathering a cluster of people do not be afraid to ask for a long-term commitment for eating together. We're not in a promise-keeping culture so commitment sounds alien and potentially cultic. This table practice will require a rugged commitment. Many live their lives with a strong dose of individualistic ADHD, transitioning to the next shiny, exciting opportunity that benefits them. We cannot be fueled by inspiration as inspiration comes and goes; we are fueled by faithful love, patterned after God's relentless faithfulness to us. Discover rootedness, converse about it, come together, and press into a long faithfulness. Consider how you can bring the table into your life every week.

The Function: Why Are We Coming Together?

Our imaginations are so temperamental. We need constant vision for why this seemingly menial practice is powerful in our lives. In our own attempt to live into shared meals we cultivate two habits: beholding one another and bearing witness to the kingdom. Beholding one another is learning to be attentive to one another, making eye contact, greeting each other warmly, asking thoughtful questions of each other, taking note of each other's postures and needs. We learn to be responsive and sensitive to each other, with the children in our midst, making overtures of welcome, and expressing appreciation for each other's participation. This shows itself in varied ways: playing with each other's kids, asking questions of curiosity about each other, remembering details from previous conversations and following up on them, celebrating each other's cultures, enjoying and affirming the goodness of each other's food dishes, reclining and learning to laugh. The other habit is bearing witness to the kingdom. This habit is one of finding ways to share what God is doing in each other's lives, naming it, affirming it, and offering encouragement to it. Hebrews 3:13 says, "Encourage one another regularly, so that none of you may be hardened by sin's deceitfulness." We are told lies daily about our worth, our roles, what will make us happy, what to be afraid of, and it all can harden us against the subversive beauty of the in-breaking kingdom. We need to learn to offer words to encourage one another. Thus we bear witness to the kingdom amongst us and around us, testifying to the alternative reality we desire to live into.

Availability and Practices

The centripetal pull for availability in community will ultimately be the practice of the table. I love the table—maybe because I love good food and good drink. I see the appearance of the table in many places throughout the narrative of Scripture. Meals are a pivotal part of the biblical narrative as the table represents the presence of God bursting into all creation when we ultimately sit at the table and dine in the new creation with Christ. To generously welcome each other at the table is to practice God's future.[3] We witness to the radically different way Jesus sees people and dwells with people. We may have turned eating at church into potlucks where we gossip about others. This is not how God in Christ approached the table. He preached the kingdom of God by the way he relaxed at the table. "Jesus came eating and drinking" (Matt 11:19). Jesus circumvented the typical use of the table in first-century culture to communicate that God was coming near. In first-century culture, feasting at the table was primarily for members of one's family. Family in its Latin sense, *familia*, covered every member of the bloodline, yet Jesus was found at the table with those not in his family. "Je-

3. Joncas, *Tasting the Reign of God*, 100–102.

sus' mother and brothers stood outside, wanting to speak to him. Someone told him, "Your mother and brothers are standing outside, wanting to speak to you." Jesus replied to him, "Who is my mother, and who are my brothers?" Pointing to his disciples, he said, "Here are my mothers and my brothers" (Mark 3:32–34). Jesus is using an enfleshed practice at the table to model and *immerse* his disciples in a new social order of family; a kingdom family. In Greek culture, beyond the familial household one might dine with the other members of one's district, class, or social origins. Freeborn Romans, for example, did not dine with former slaves. The heads of the aristocracy invited other aristocrats to banquet with each other. Social rules of dining mirrored the sectarian structures of the first century in both Judaism and Greco-Roman life. Deciding who you could eat with was a serious matter, yet Jesus uses the table to flip boundaries of insiders and outsiders.[4] He ate with people in the neighborhood as evidenced when the Pharisees asked with snark, "Why does he eat with tax collectors and sinners?" What is Jesus saying in his table practices? And what does it say about his followers? As for the Greeks and for the Jews of Jesus' day, meals today are much more than nutrition. They bound participants to one another by covenants established at the table. Jesus' meal practices contested, transformed, and reinterpreted everything.[5] Jesus cultivated community at the table, modeling other-worldly availability. The Last Supper stands as the pinnacle of a new pattern of being in the world. Jesus reclined at the table with doubters, cowards, and betrayers and called them friends. Jesus shared the table as a pointer to the "fulfillment in the kingdom of God" (Luke 14:16). Eating together becomes a dynamic way we make ourselves available to God and to each other. We foreshadow the feast at the table when the kingdom of God is fully realized (Rev 19:9). Ultimately our availability to each other flows from the eucharistic table displayed for us when Jesus says "this is my body . . . this is my blood." The church confesses the real, living presence of Jesus in the Eucharist. The spirit of God breathes life into these physical acts of placing the bread of Christ into our mouth and feeling the wine of Christ on our tongue. This sacrament becomes a formative event for our bodies, our minds, and our collective presence with each other. The Eucharist can become an empty ritual or a hip novelty without imagination for how Jesus' presence shapes a localized people. It pulls us into covenant, into community, into an outpost for the kingdom of God. We must cultivate presence;

4. Baltimore Lutheran Ministry, "The Revolutionary Table."
5. Joncas, *Tasting the Reign of God,* 100–102.

it does not just happen to us. A piece of furniture is not present in a room, it is simply there.[6] People can be in the same room with each other, attend the same event and partake in the same information without being present to each other. Our churches can easily condition us to be objects, like furniture, simply there but not present. The Eucharist rattles our bones; awakening us to the mystical way the Holy Spirit frolics amongst our souls. The profound reality is that we are supernaturally fed and transformed when we gather together at the eucharistic table. We become a eucharistic community that is sourced from the food and fountain of Jesus himself. "'I am the living bread, come down from heaven,' said Christ: 'those who eat this bread shall have Kingdom life; and the bread I give is my flesh for the life of the world. . . . Whoever eats my flesh and drinks my blood will be given life'" (John 6:51). It is out of this nourishment that we can nourish others. It is because God sacrificed himself in self-emptying love that we can make deep sacrifices in practical love for each other. God's presence at the table is not a *thing*, it is an exercise in being present to God despite how distant he may feel at times, and being present to each other despite how different we are. We are rallied together and reminded at the table of the way of God in Christ. Something real occurs in the bread and wine that establishes our identity as a community born from above. Because the Eucharist is our centering sacrament, our formation for community becomes a sacrament. This eucharistic table is our primary shaping rhythm that informs our eating with others in the rest of our Monday-through-Saturday lives. The table has the same mysterious power today as it did in New Testament times.

The dining room table throughout history has been the means for brokering treaties between countries. It has been used in harmful ways to alienate slaves and women. It has been the place where enemies have come together in peace and it is the place where loads of homework is done. The table is an explosive piece of furniture, used in humanizing and dehumanizing ways. Though the legacy has grown over the years, the modest kitchen table continues to be a center of activity. Even before electricity found its way into American homes, the kitchen table would be used for homework and numerous other household tasks. Meals were prepared there, children were taught there, and families grew and matured there. Considering how much time early American families spent gathered around this basic structure, it's no wonder that people continue to feel drawn to the table. It doesn't take a psychology degree to see why—people are forced

6. Thurian, *The Mystery of the Eucharist*, 52.

to relationally collide at it. The table beckons people to gather around and sit a little closer to each other than they normally would. In this day and age many forces are pulling and tugging at us—busy schedules, demanding jobs, and fast food. The table works to bring us back together in the midst of the tsunami of frenzied activity and isolation. The tidal wave of our electronic culture is changing traditional notions of meals and this is transforming human interaction. A growing number of people are not seeing the meal as a central activity for communication. Eating at a table with others is losing its place in our lives. It's just one of several activities being overrun by involvement with computers and smartphones, including surfing the Web and communicating with friends via Facebook. This does not mean we are any less social, we're just interacting less with people in real time. Socialization is more via avatars than physical presence. Much research has been done on how meal time at the table shapes child development. On average, 40 percent of families surveyed nationally report they eat together about three times per week.[7] Developmental scientists have detected a radical risk reduction in children who gather around the table three or more times a week for dinner; they are less likely to smoke cigarettes or use marijuana and are at reduced risk of abusing alcohol,[8] are less likely to develop eating disorders as preteens,[9] more likely to graduate high school,[10] and have fewer emotional problems.[11] The kitchen table should be the vortex for family life. There is something elemental in all this research. Tables create togetherness, teach us to take time to talk, and help prevent our relationships from withering and dying. If being at the table is good for the souls of children, I've got to believe it's also necessary for the souls of adults under the onslaught of twenty-first-century life. And just as table practice has faded in nuclear families, it has all but disintegrated in forming community beyond family. Jesus piloted this practice. Shared meal times is an immensely symbolic event, a barometer for community. Something sacramental and sacred occurs as we commit to coming together.

My wife and I have sought to foster availability through the means of the table. The dining room table has become a great force in our lives, opening up space for refugees, sojourners, good friends, and neighbors. As

7. Bradley and Corwyn, "Child Trends," 375.

8. Ibid., 377.

9. Ibid., 378.

10. Ibid., 380.

11. Ibid., 381.

we eat, we organically share our highs and lows, assembling a natural nest to hatch new exchanges between us. We change the climate of our community as we lean into a pattern of eating together regularly. We aggregate our stories to build a whole new story filled with memories and meaning. At that regular practice of sharing the table we are catching a glimpse of the kingdom tree sprouting up and offering shade and belonging for us all. Cook your food together, bring dishes to pass, welcome the noise that kids bring, celebrate Lent, experiment with meals from other countries, share about your week, listen to a written prayer, pray for each other, pray for your neighbors. The kingdom of God is paved with conversations that overlap our lives. The rhythmic pattern of gathering around the table molds our stubborn bodies and stuffed schedules into a circle of discipleship. We are fashioned into something new as we linger with others, overriding our natural tendency toward seeing food as tool for self-indulgence and rather seeing it as a sacred centripetal pull towards each other. The table stands for a place of deep divine availability in the wilderness of isolating, fragmenting American life. We're invited into the life of God, not as a museum, not as a march, but as a meal around a table with Jesus leading the conversation. The renewal of the church will not start on stages, it will start around our tables.

Availability and Partnering

Increased availability is a track we ride on towards depths of *partnership* for the kingdom of God. Availability is a mutual effort. Availability can be exceptionally frustrating without a context of commitment. This might sound a bit funny, but flawed availability in community is bit like a young woman who feels deep frustration because she's unsure of her boyfriend's level of commitment. She is unsure if her efforts are in vain. The fellow may (or may not) have commitment issues. This makes the relationship confusing, fuzzy, and unstable. This emotional uncertainty occurs in community formation when commitment is sketchy. We cannot cultivate roots with each other with an easy on- and off-ramp mentality. We're often frightened by commitment, feeling it constrains us. So we try to relate at arm's length. This form of relating creates expectations that will inevitably be dashed. It also assumes pure responsibility on the part of one party in the community to be strong enough to do most of the heavy lifting. We must call each other to commitment to mutual *partnership*. This is not about control; it's about trust that we will not abandon each other when we become bored, offended, or tired of each other. I cannot stress enough how love is translated to people in terms of commitment. For as much as we run from commitment we still expect it from others. Community has the tendency to open up chaos in our souls as it calls us to relate in unselfish ways. We will be surprised by our compulsions to flee when our self-orientation is challenged. Certainly we all have seasons when we are "needy." I've have had those seasons as I was unable to initiate availability, and yet grace was extended to me. This is why partnering together is essential to reshape our wandering spirits. Partnership is the pledge of mutual commitment for mutual work of building up the kingdom of God. Partnership brings us out of the dark agony of caving on ourselves. Availability begins to rehumanize us to the needs and abundance in each other.[12] We begin to see ordinary points of contact as significant. Our work to scooch closer to each other opens us up to new life-giving loyalties. We learn to be together, warts, eccentricities, irritants and all. This is very ordinary but essential, which can challenge explorers who are tempted to dip their toe in the water and then find a more thrilling experience elsewhere.[13] We must not project the idea that our relationships are expendable. Partnering for availability is not about taking things to the next level but taking each other's humanity seriously. Resist the pressure to push things faster. We don't build rhythms of availability with each other to deliver double-digit returns on the growth of our numerical attendance. When people sense that becoming available to each other has a hurried anxiety underpinning it for the sake of a target, they begin to feel like pieces for a project. The key to creating a life-giving community is to see the power in the small but important element of being with others; this creates a crack in our garrisoned selves. What makes availability complex is that it occurs in an infinite number of small sacrifices and most often in quiet gestures.[14] We must embrace patience with our attachments, seeking slowness as a route to depth. You cannot rush the return of availability. It takes time since people are not gears to be turned. Forming availability with each other is not a paint-by-numbers kit. Our urgency is often attached to our grandiose expectations. We all come to community importing our visions of how it should operate. In my last fifteen years of cultivating community I've discovered how difficult it is for people to even verbalize those expectations,

12. Block, *Community*, 78–79.

13. Pohl, *Living Into Community*, 90–93.

14. Janzen, *The Intentional Christian Community*, 140–45.

so they go unsaid until they bottle up and explode. Idealism comes from a lack of saturation and suffering in application, clinging to the abstract. We can read, study, and talk all day about how community *should* function, but at the moment it actually occurs it is forced to negotiate the tension of real people with real messiness. There is no utopian community, which is why it's important to expose our dysfunctional fantasies. Patience puts our demands on the operating table. Patience is more than waiting, it is the ability to linger with people for *who* they are and *where* they are. It teaches us to value each other in the moment rather than valuing each other for how we want things to go. Patience teaches that people are not tools to be possessed for our own emotional needs and that they are not projects for us to fix. In building rhythms of availability we can transcend the narrative of anxiety as we choose security over insecurity with others also patiently committed to the process. Those feelings of bondedness do come at a manageable pace. We just need to embrace the pace. The slowness of developing availability challenges our patience but it is the slowness that cultivates careful seeds in the soil of our existence.

VULNERABILITY

"Walk in the light as he is in the light and we will have fellowship with one another" (1 John 1:7). Notice this "lighting" process is about having better fellowship with each other. Allowing light in is not a pietistic pursuit but a pursuit of becoming healthier people together. Vulnerability in community leads us to incrementally present ourselves as we are, limited, afraid, insecure, angry, weak, excited. We are so prone to protection, posing and powering up, but honesty is the only remedy for peering past the accessories of our life. Vulnerability is a doorway to transformation, allowing the sun's rays into the rooms of our heart. Vulnerability is experienced as moments of emotional strength, not weakness. It is strength because at the moment we're vulnerable we let go of our silly illusions that we can control our image.

Vulnerability and Dignity

Wherever I've traveled in the world I've found there is an aching center in us all to be given dignity. Few people understand the true meaning of dignity, and even fewer realize the extraordinary role it plays in community.

Most people think dignity means respect. Dignity goes way beyond that. Dignity is our inherent value and worth as human beings. God has crafted us all unique as our temperaments are different, our histories are different, and our personalities are different. We are prone to apply value to people that we share the most in common with and who are *like* us. When we discover malformations, oddities, and irritants we pull back on communicating value, we withhold offering dignity. This was precisely what inflamed Paul so much that he confronted Peter. "Later, when Peter came to Antioch, I had a face-to-face confrontation with him because he was clearly out of line. Here's the situation. Earlier, Peter regularly ate with the non-Jews. But when that conservative group came from Jerusalem, he cautiously pulled back and put as much distance as he could manage between himself and his non-Jewish friends. Unfortunately, the rest of the Jews in the Antioch church joined in his behavior as others were swept along in the charade" (Gal 2:11–13). With some passive aggressive tactics, Peter pulled back on his acceptance of his non-Jewish friends. He communicated a lack of dignity to them. We have a shared desire for dignity that needs to transcend all of our differences, putting our common human identity above all else. We are all ordinary and fragile and there is deep danger in forgetting this. While our uniqueness is important, history has shown that if we don't take the next step toward recognizing our shared identity, divisions will abound between us. To offer dignity we need a supernatural work of grace in our heart to push beyond what we like or dislike on the surface. Just as Jesus offers dignity to persons, we are to reenact this unusual affirmation of the human soul. Jesus modeled the truth that every person has an underlying goodness, created in God's image. We may like this in theory but we chafe when push comes to shove. When we see a glimmer of something annoying in our brother or sister in Christ we have a tendency to take a step backwards. We are sly about organizing a plan to avoid and distance. We must rebuke this distorted impulse. In the work of vulnerability we must offer each other deep dignity rather than fake affection.

Sometimes our resistance is related to our own insecurity. We are always tempted to cover up like Adam and Eve, using whatever covering we can find: our eloquence, our intellect, our position of power, the books we've read, our evasiveness, our sarcasm, our business success. We find ourselves guarding ourselves, trying to maintain an appearance with others. We inevitability treat others the way we treat ourselves, comparing and contrasting who we are against their presented image. People dazzle us with their gifts so we try to dazzle them with ours. We look to rank ourselves, scanning the room for "Who is my equal?" We love to tell ourselves "I'm not as bad as *they* are." But there is no divine Richter scale ranking whose sins are less than others.[15] When we believe there is, we become the deities in our own little mental empires, handing out verdicts on others' value. We are all tempted to suppress anything that would threaten our guru image but we must take an axe to that emotional tower. In one of Jesus' weakest moments in the garden of Gethsemane, he does something foolish in the school of "being strong." Jesus invites Peter, James, and John in close to behold his struggle.[16] Jesus pioneers space for others to witness his knee-knocking fragility. "Father, I'm afraid, could you please take this cup from me?" (Luke 22:42). Jesus is embarrassingly vulnerable. Don't domesticate what Jesus did. In our culture this would be called "seeing someone at their worst." Jesus was exposing disciples to the drama of his own humbling. The wisdom of this is hidden from leadership experts. There is an agony in Christlike vulnerability. We're all weak; most of us are just too afraid to admit it. To participate in Christ takes a sledgehammer to our superiority and allows us to find dignity in each other as we are.

Vulnerability and Delight

Vulnerability invites the opportunity to delight in one another as God loves to delight in people. God speaks these words to Jesus: "You are my beloved in whom I am pleased" (Mark 1:11). We are tasked with transmitting those words to each other. To delight is to celebrate each other, to revel in the wildly distinct ways we are crafted. To delight we must slay our teeth-gritted resistance to enjoying people that are not clones of ourselves.

Inadequacy and Cynicism

There are two hidden impulses that prevent us from delighting in others: inadequacy and cynicism.[17] Inadequacy tells us that the truest thing about us is our deficiencies, our ugly spots, our performance, or our victimhood. So we listen to our mind's voices that say "hold back," "you are not wanted

---

15. Pohl, *Living Into Community*, 33–35.

16. White Jr., "Sabotaging the Hero Complex."

17. Block, *Community*, 80–81.

here," and forget many in our community internally feel the same way. When we become myopic about our own inadequacy we unknowingly project rejection to others, giving energy to the cycle of distance from each other. Cynicism on the other hand is always suspicious, telling us to "weigh other options" and "keep some space." We may hold bitterness that no one honors us the way we want to be honored, so we retreat into disdain. It must become a spiritual discipline to look for the good in people buried beneath the pettiness, resentments, and ambitions that irritate us about each other.[18] Thomas á Kempis has said, "There is no creature, regardless of its apparent insignificance, that fails to show us something of God's goodness."[19] The grace of God reminds us we are all a mixture of destructive impulses and powerfully life-giving impulses, loving like Jesus one day and sinning like the devil the next. We certainly do meet the best and worst in ourselves in community. We learn that we don't have to remake everyone in our own image to love them. We must actively resist the smoke and mirrors that tell us to write someone off for an irritating action. Instead, mine for gold in the cave of each other's hearts and learn to delight in each other's differences. Verbalize your acknowledgments of each other; do not be conservative with your enjoyment of others. "We loved you so much; we were delighted to share our lives with you" (1 Thess 2:8). Do not be trite, be genuine in letting yourself give your heart to the joy of others' company. Extroverts and introverts will do this differently but it must typify our life together. People do not sustain vulnerability with each other without being able to imagine that their community enjoys who they are. As the trinitarian God was able to look at the first humans and say "it is good," we must work towards this same culture with each other.

Vulnerability and Disclosure

Disclosure is the act of making something known that was not previously known. Disclosure allows us to survey who we are and who we're becoming, exposing the myths we hold about ourselves. These spaces require questions, feedback, honesty, contemplation, active listening, eye contact, confession, and accountability. "Where two or three of us are gathered" God is among us (Matt 18:20). Within discipleship in Jesus' day, it was in the smaller space of *midrash* where disclosure was often practiced. In

18. Janzen, *The Intentional Christian Community*, 140–45.

19. Kempis, *The Imitation of Christ*, 88.

Judaism, during midrash, apprentices of a teacher would gather around after a public teaching on Scripture to fill in gaps, resolve problems, unearth
implications, and move beyond rhetorical skills.[20] The primitive root of
midrash is the Hebrew word *darash*, which means to seek, search, or yearn
for understanding. The midrash approach encourages gut-level "yearning
and searching" before drawing conclusions—seeking understanding about
what God is saying through our wrestling. The majority of the Gospels'
written words are captured from the actual environments of midrash, with
the large teaching environments being more the exception. What we read
is the community's collective memory of learning and discussing with Jesus
on the streets, on the mountainside, around meals, or at a campfire. The
rabbi Jesus had no interest in having students spit back information just for
the sake of appearances.[21] We need spaces where assessing the voice of God
is not a one way delivery system; we need space to "work out our salvation"
(Phil 2:12).

Galatians 6:4 reads, "Let everyone examine together the work they've
accomplished, for then you can delight in the work of your hands without
pride. Do not compare yourselves with each other; rather seek God's help
in making the inner secrets of your hearts plain; that way we can work
on what God is doing in us." This verse inspired the Jesuit practice of the
examen of consciousness, founded 500 years ago. It was an done to explore
motivations, hopes, and failures. It was a confessional space. Dietrich Bonhoeffer said in his glorious book *Life Together*, "When we confess our sin to
a fellow believer, we are no longer alone, we experience the presence of God
between us."[22] Learning to leverage the value of such examination should
erect a sacred space between you and a few others in your community. In
my experience, there have been many times at a coffee shop, on a front
stoop, or walking with a neighbor that a holy temple was created in our
conversation. Communal examination is essential for maturing together
and even for our own nourishment. We're in a time when Christians are
being shaped more by celebrity preachers, the latest book, and social media
than by mutual discipleship. We need fresh, updated ways to honor the
spirit of ancient midrash and the traditional practice of examen. We need
cross-pollinational pods that encourage discourse and disclosure that leans
towards realigning our desires under God's reign in Jesus. Information

20. Hammer, *The Classic Midrash*, 17–18.

21. Chalke, *Apprentice*, 21–22.

22. Bonhoeffer, *Life Together*, 57–58.

hardly ever moves to practice if it is not discovered within this space of vulnerability.

Out of this passionate desire of discipleship pods within community we must have a framework for understanding the discipleship relationship, hence the belonging and becoming matrix.

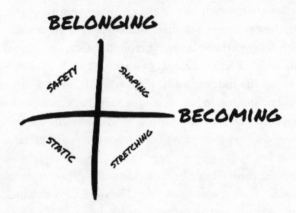

Belonging and Becoming Matrix

When you begin to break down the punishing doctrine of individualism you must establish some new scaffolding for discipleship. We will always be individuals but we must choose to reorient around an interdependent life rather than an independent one. The discipling relationships must have scaffolding that helps us orient who we are with each other. In my experience there are two social constructs that are separate but should intersect with each other. These social bearings should not be hidden supports but move into the explicit as we name them and wrestle with our embrace of them. They are belonging and becoming.

BELONGING

To belong with a handful of others is perhaps the most important and least recognized need of the human soul. Belonging is the space within a discipleship relationship where we begin to feel it is safe to be ourselves. Belonging is social support to the degree that our basic social needs are met through time spent with specific people. Belonging happens when the resources of intangible emotional support and tangible physical presence begin to grow between people. Whether we admit it or not, at the nexus of our identity is an ongoing crisis of worth. Are we valuable? Are we wanted? Are we loved? Are we welcome here? Are we understood? Relying solely on God is not New Testament Christianity; it's American Christianity. We must press hard into belonging or we cannot comprehend and materialize our identity as disciples. Belonging creates a landing spot for our life. To build a sense of belonging requires active effort and practice. One way to work on increasing your sense of belonging is to look for ways you are similar to others instead of focusing on how you are different. Maybe someone older has wise stories to tell and you love to listen to their experiences. Maybe some have a different opinions on issues than you but you enjoy learning from another perspective and can embrace each other as brothers and sisters in Christ. Sharing your differences and still accepting the person creates space for belonging. Acceptance does not mean assimilation into uniformity. To desire acceptance might seem like an adolescent need, but I have yet to meet an adult who has outgrown this often unspoken desire. Our cohesiveness comes from the disciplined work of extending belonging to each other. The outcome of belonging is safety, safety to present ourselves as we are. The more safety our soul feels the less danger we feel about the instability of the discipleship relationship. Without belonging in discipleship you are more akin to a business contract rather than a bonded relationship. In any discipleship relationship, the content of what is learned is a bit less important than the relationship itself. It is prolonged presence that communicates what is essential.

At least two things undercut belonging in a discipleship relationship:

Distancing

When we are together we protect ourselves from being known by projecting a certain preferred image. Maybe we speak in generalities or say we are feeling good when we are not. We may play hard to get, sending signals of distance. This can be communicated by averted eyes and a less-than-warm greetings. Each individual must unwrap when and how they keep a distance. Some keep a distance because they want to keep up appearances, others because intimacy is unfamiliar and awkward.

Distrust

Maybe we've been hurt in the past or maybe we are just suspicious. The response then might be to tell ourselves not to entrust ourselves too much to anyone. This can exhaust the discipling relationship. This becomes cyclical when in so many ways we communicate distrust and others become hesitant to trust us. Cultivating trust is not automatic but it must be a spoken intent.

Belonging is vital in discipling relationships. Safety is essential but over time will slip into static. We cannot simply choose safety and stay there indefinitely. Often when there has been a strong deficit in belonging in our life, we long to cling to this status without movement. We must together understand that belonging is only one aspect of a fruitful discipleship relationship. We cannot solely seek asylum with each other. We must seek action.

BECOMING

To become with others is to embark on a journey towards transformation. This becoming acknowledges there are parts of me that need more renewing than others. The walk towards maturing in Christ cannot be made in isolation; we cannot understand ourselves outside of a localized, accountable community. Sadly, most of our formation takes place through disembodied connections: social media, books, podcasts, etc. In our commitment to an embodied discipleship we exercise muscles that we want to avoid using but that make us more nimble Jesus-followers. We must seek to explore the raw material that forms the essence of who we are, excavating our motivations and stimulating fresh activity. We seek to be stretched. The organic apparatus for stretching begins with better questions of examen. We prime the pump for stretching as we "spur one another on to love and good actions" (Heb 10:24). Admit it, we've become quite sophisticated at photoshopping ourselves. So we must look in the mirror. This can feel like a scalpel and a warm cup of tea at the same time. In my own discipleship pods we rotate between three questions:

1. *"What is God doing in me?"*
This question calls us to pay attention to what is clanking around in our heart, seeking self-knowledge about the Holy Spirit's careful surgery taking

place within us. This helps us to reflect, record, and respond to God's Spirit in our life.

2. *"What is God doing around me?"*

We realize our relationships need careful attention and God uses this question for speaking to us and exposing what hurt feelings we've been nursing. God also uses community to expose our judgments, hatreds, and callousness toward people. Who am I challenged to love? Where am I experiencing conflict?

3. *"What is God doing through me?"*

Explore the unique missional ministry God is inviting us into. Who is God calling us to incarnate with, to be present with, to sacrifice for? How are we loving our neighbors? Are we consistent?

Two things that undercut becoming in discipleship relationships:

Deflection

Accepting stretching doesn't mean you set yourself up to be a verbal punching bag for anyone to strike. Accepting stretching through feedback and challenge really means holding your tongue, your emotions, and your natural inclinations long enough to listen so that you can give yourself the opportunity for self-reflection. Deflection finds ways to dodge this process and cushion the blunt contact of constructive criticism or blatant application of something new.

Denial

We are so sold on our interpretation of who we are and what we are, we cannot conceive that we may be viewed by others in a considerably different light. Denial sometimes occurs because we are more attuned to our own egos than to our desire for inner growth.

With the convergence of belonging and becoming we have a combination of safety and stretching in our discipleship relationship. This leads to *shaping*, an ongoing slow hike towards our personhood being formed. We can diagnose our discipleship relationship with this matrix. We ask ourselves if we are situated primarily in belonging, seeking safety, or primarily in becoming, seeking to be stretched. A flourishing discipleship relationship cultivates soil with both fertilizers.

RELATIONAL TETHERING TOOL

Years ago I joined up with a friend to do some rock climbing. I was a novice but he wasn't. He had invested quite a bit money into good gear to climb and rappel. I had learned that a climber's gear is highly valued. Their gear is their investment which provides them the wild occasion to hang from 100-foot cliffs. One Sunday afternoon we set out to explore a new space to climb in the mountains of southern Pennsylvania. We found the base of a cliff. We began to open up the backpacks that held the gear—pulling out helmets, gloves, carabiners, and ropes. My friend began inspecting everything and something caught his eye. He knelt down closer to look at one of the ropes. He lifted up the rope, showing me what he'd discovered. The rope had begun to fray in the middle. A rope is a fabric of individual strands tethered together to form one cord. When it frays those strands start to pull apart, weakening the rope. My friend was disappointed and stated "the rope is frayed and is too thin to hold the weight of our climbing." Years later, I remember that concept and think of it metaphorically: *the rope is not strong enough; it is too thin to hold the weight of our work.*

Making a Rope

A rope is a bundle of flexible fibers twisted or braided together to increase its overall length and tensile strength. Tensile strength is a unique strength that can handle large amounts of weight but is also flexible enough to provide some spring. Rope construction involves twisting fibers together to form strands and those strands are then twisted into rope. Three-strand twisted rope is the most common construction and is still the strongest and most durable weave for creating a rope. For community we need a three-corded rope. Ecclesiastes 4:9–12 points out the power of a three-stranded rope in the context of community. "Multiples are better than one, because they have a good return for their labor: If one falls down, another can help the other up. But pity anyone who falls and has no one to help them up. How can one keep warm alone? Though one may be overpowered, together they can defend themselves. A cord of three strands is not quickly broken." Community in practice is the tethering of lives that thickens a life together as a sign of the in-breaking kingdom of God. The cord of community must be thick enough to bear the weight of our missional work in the world. Relational tethering is cultivating a sustainable shared life. We need to learn how to diagnose frays in community and cultivate better relational habits. Through healthy relational-emotional habits we form a fabric together: thin to thick community. Our aim is a thicker community life. We must help people recognize and resolve what hinders community, if we do not we tend to unravel.

The following relational tethering tool is a framework for discussion, diagnosis, and discipleship that, when taught and employed in community, can cast fresh light on complexities and offer us opportunities for maturing. *Relational tethering involves cords braided together that thicken and enrich our availability and vulnerability in community.*

Trust-Building = *habits that foster stability instead of suspicion.*

The health of human bonds depends on relational glue that holds us together. Our connectedness is constantly under duress. We must tend to our bonds, naming what contributes to stability. Often we enter into a community flush with ideals that will be humbled in the work of bonding with people. This bond forming is the work of trust-building. There are unexplainable gaps between what we expect people to do and what they actually do.[23] What we choose to place in those gaps determines the strength and integrity of the relationships. We can choose to fill them with suspicion but this erodes our relational ties with each other. Our histories of failed relationships can torque us towards ongoing suspicion. The wounds we have experienced, some very deep, have shaped our souls. In our inability to cope with these wounds, we often revert to wounding other people in similar ways. "Do not bite and devour one another or you will be devoured by evil yourselves" (Gal 5:15). To overcome the cycle of suspicion that erodes relationships we must seek to defer to trust. Maturing as a disciple is learning to be still when you want to be defensive. When we see something

23. Stanley, *Trust vs. Suspicion.*

concerning we must always lean towards finding out more directly from the person in question. Obviously it is impossible to grant unilateral trust to people immediately. Rather we must work toward installing trust that leads to increasing trust.

Thick Community (Stability) = *cultivating strong bonds with each other.*

- Do we deliver on what we say we are going to do?

- Do we say sorry when we cannot follow through?

- Do we forgive when people ask for grace?

- Do we seek to cut others slack in their motives as we do for ourselves?

- Is communication related to unmet expectations done face-to-face?

- Is it okay to fail?

- Do we express faithfulness to each other?

- Do we put effort into relationships that begin to break down?

Thin Community (Suspicion) = *casting doubt on each other.*

- Do we respect direct channels of communication?

- Do we have a tendency to attribute negative motives to people's intentions before speaking with them?

- Do we fill in the blanks of someone's reputation when there is a sense of doubt?

- Do we speak passive-aggressively about people when we are disappointed with them?

- Do we abandon relationships that seem difficult to maintain?

- Do we hide big choices we're making (vocation, dating, moving, etc.)?

- When someone is gone do we call them? When someone is sick do we visit them?

- When someone is different in opinion and culture, do we avoid them?

- When something better comes along, will I leave?

Truth-Telling = *habits that foster honesty instead of hiding.*

For most this is unnavigated social terrain. "Put away falsehood with each other, remembering that we belong to one another" (Eph 4:25). What does truth-shaped living look like? For most, speaking the truth has appeared more like a caricature of a preacher yelling "truth" at us from a stage. Or we confuse discontented grumbling with truth-telling. Bluntness is not the same as truthfulness. Truth-telling is first speaking the truth about ourselves before pointing out the speck in someone else's eye.[24] A truth-telling community will not necessarily be tidy because rough edges are allowed to be seen. Truth-telling seeks to first understand before unloading an opinion. Environments of truth-telling seek to be honest and direct with who we are and what we're feeling. Direct speech brings clarity and keeps manipulation and hiding at bay.[25] Cultures of community that do not permit frank speech often hide under the surface resentments, abuses, and stifled feelings. Too often we Christians switch between passive silence and bitter tirades in the face of differences. We must work slavishly to practice a better way. Frank speech does not seek injury. Truth-telling communities must become wise to the way passive-aggressive communication festers. It is passive because one adopts the position of someone acted upon or injured, and it is aggressive because one grasps for power and control in this arrangement, in that one forces another person into the position of malevolent injurer.[26] A passive-aggressive person grasps after power over another person by judging his motives without direct, open communication. The relational strategy is indirect, so their anger cannot be identified but is still felt. Pure passivity is not virtuous either, assuming that when someone insults us the virtuous

24. Tucker, *Uncovered,* 44–45.
25. Crabb, *Connecting,* 67–68.
26. Gombis, "Passive Aggressive Postures."

thing to do is nothing. Passive relating tends not to say anything in the moment of hurt but later vomits on someone unrelated. Genuine love does not delight in evil but rejoices with the truth. We must throw a flag when we see relating that is untruthful, perpetuating the nursing of wounds, angry inner tirades, and postures that are less than genuine.[27] Truthfulness is a cord that holds us together in a world of dishonest relating.

Thick Community *(Honesty)* = *seeking sincerity with others.*

- Do we speak frankly when we are offended?

- Do we speak well of others when they're not in our presence?

- How do we dismantle pretending and posing in our relationships?

- Have we communicated an open posture to hearing truth-speak from another?

- Do we fear speaking the truth to certain people?

- Do we seek to look at the planks in our own eyes before picking at others' specks?

- How do we give people permission to share openly?

Thin Community *(Hiding)* = *masking or misrepresenting who I am.*

- When we are upset do we avoid?

- Do we practice triangulating or gossip?

- Do we sit and stroke our offenses until they separate us?

- Do we use anti-relational media (email, Twitter, etc.) to communicate sensitive thoughts?

- Do we protect a distorted image of ourselves?

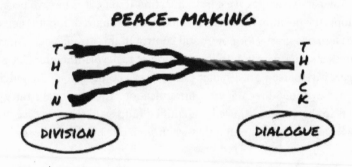

27. Pohl, *Living Into Community*, 51–52.

Peace-making = *habits that foster dialogue instead of division.*

We are to be "ministers of reconciliation" (2 Cor 5:18). This has become more of a catchphrase than a serious pursuit in Christian circles. To be human is to have differences. In community we will be faced with processing those differences. The temptation is to bail or divide from community when conflict overtakes us. We must seek out reconciling dialogue instead. Conflict is helpful for forming us, causing us to attend to new insight on each other.[28] Relational intimacy requires conflict. The work of peace-making is not sweeping hurts, disappointments, and angers under the carpet—this only increases the potential for carnage. I have been in too many churches where individuals and factions of people do not talk directly to each other, preferring to accumulate offenses into a mound that seems insurmountable. Some seek to build up a power base of support to gain ammunition against their offender and others boil internally, eventually departing without ever having a face-to-face conversation. The path of peace will open up conversations about what is going on in an attempt to shed redemptive light on the situation. Conflict can be a useful opportunity, calling us to behold new perspectives that can transform us. "As far as it depends on you live at peace with each other" (Rom 12:18). When we stretch to contend for the purpose of reconciliation it is not merely a human activity but a matter of binding on earth what is bound in heaven (Matt 18:18). The Anabaptist tradition has historically called this "binding and loosing," seeing it as a sacrament identifying the church in distinction from the world.[29] We are to go to each other in a spirit of gentleness in awareness of our own weakness.[30] Conversation with reconciling intent is the most powerful way for a community to discover God's spirit in our midst. I find it striking that in the midst of the conflict in Corinth Paul never instructed readers to leave the community to find a healthier one. Instead, he instructed them to work it out. We are not a community if we cannot move into conflict and move through it while maintaining our loyal love for one another. We must press into conflict with fidelity, not rigidity.[31] Peace-makers are the children of God.

Thick Community (Dialogue) = seeking conversation in times of conflict.

28. Dana, *Conflict Resolution*, 62–64.
29. Yoder, *Body Politics*, 14–15.
30. Ibid., 16.
31. Ibid., 17.

- How do we create a "sit down and talk" culture?
- Do we permit someone to stretch us without deforming us?
- Are we quick to listen and slow to speak? Slow to be defensive?
- Do we seek solidarity through questioning, seeking to understand?
- Do we allow conflict to become the occasion for our growth?
- Do we forgive and release someone who says sorry?
- Can we live patiently with differences that are not yet resolved?
- Do we seek reconciliation or separation first?

Thin Community (Division) = *coming into collision that perpetuates separation.*

- Do we add toxicity to disagreement by throwing people's reputations under the bus?
- Do we fight or flee?
- Do we build up a power base of support so that we can win?
- Do we shut out people who have a different take?
- If I am wronged am I able to own my faults?
- Do I perpetuate the hurt done to me by being retributive?
- Do I communicate rejection when someone has an issue with me?
- When we let someone down do we hope that no one notices?

Conclusion

IN OUR LITTLE URBAN side yard my wife has been nursing two small bonsai trees. They are intriguing and interesting trees to look at. They are delicate plants that require lots of attention and care. You don't just throw them in the ground and let them do their thing, especially in the harsh elements of the Northeast. Because we live in the frigid cold for five months a year my wife has to carefully pull up those trees, pot them, shelter them through winter, and bring them back out in the early spring. Her patience with those trees challenges me because I would have given up on them already. When she pulls them up, it's the roots that she meticulously tends to. Each root is essential so she isolates them, draws them up slowly and brushes them off gently. When she replants the bonsai every year I say "I hope they make it" and every year she says "They will because the roots are good." I'm learning to believe with her that the most interesting and beautiful things take patience, practice, and a lot of presence. There's no drive-through window for growing something meaningful. There's no Miracle-Gro for making something that matters. The only things that grow fast in nature are weeds, mold, and fungus.[32]

Maybe you've been following the bread crumbs that the future of church is subterranean, a radical-rootedness. Let that stir up wonder in you, but let it lead your conversations, calling others into community and into the cause of your neighborhood. You might face a stadium of doubters but all reformations begin on the edges. They are sparked when a few people are committed to a new path, a marginal way forward. The Servant-King Jesus is with us as we follow in his wake to carve out a new way to be human, a new social order under his reign. Don't be afraid of the future as we come upon the world with its technocratic demands arrayed against our

---

32. Comment on my blog, danwhitejr.blogspot.com, from Matt O.

rebellious weapons of incarnation. Being a subterranean church is not a distant utopian fantasy, even though it is the narrow way.

Eugene Peterson has said, "The most effective strategy for change, for revolution—at least on the large scale that the Kingdom of God involves—comes from a minority working from the margins. . . . A minority people working from the margins has the best chance of being a community capable of penetrating the non-community, the mob, the de-personalized, function-defined crowd that is the sociological norm of America."[33] They might already be people in your city seeking a radically rooted expression of the church. Maybe you need to wrestle furiously with God's Spirit about whether you should gather people together for this purpose. Don't let the celestial monsters within and without frighten you into inaction. There is no greater work than building a Tree of Life in a place. Right out in my front yard I have huge honey locust tree. There's a strong urge for new life, new entrepreneurs, and new money to enter into our blue-collar city. I understand why. We need to press into the future. Yet when I look at that tree, its thick trunk and its creeping roots pressing up and cracking the sidewalk, I fear for its life. I fear that in our surge towards the new, we'll steamroll over what roots us, what offers us stability and nourishment. I'm an innovator and I'm drawn to creative ways to remedy problems, but in pressing into the future we need to reach into our primordial past for inspiration, for orientation, for wisdom, for guidance. To respect the rootage of the past and simultaneously see further into the future, I've climbed that tree in my front yard, as cars race by and fast-paced pedestrians stare up as if they're seeing a foreign activity. In our city you don't climb trees; you play video games. What would it look like for the church to become a subterranean movement again? What would it look like to have eyes to see the supernatural significance of radically rooting to plant a Tree of Life in our neighborhoods? Seek counsel, find community, and submerge.

33. Peterson, *The Pastor*, 56–58.

Afterword

For Christians living in North America today, these are the strangest of times. When it comes to church, the rules have all changed. Everything we learned about evangelism, worship services, and discipleship forty years ago (for those of us who are that old) seems no longer to apply. The culture has changed and we're searching for new ways to be the church. But, at this point in the upheaval of Western culture, we do not need a new cool way to do church. We need an entire new way of life. Allow me to explain.

Most of us learned church by "going to church." We learned early to center the Christian part of our lives around attending a worship service on Sundays. The rest of our lives would develop from there. We would serve on some committees or boards whenever possible. We would take part in various evangelistic initiatives to engage with people outside the church, most of whom we had never met before. We would volunteer at the local soup kitchen to help "the poor," most of who lived miles away from the places where we lived. Back then, we saw no need to intersect relationally with our neighbors, our surrounding culture, or the hurting people around the corner from our church building. If any of them wanted God, they could simply "go to church" like us.

Somehow this worked when the majority of the culture was Christianized. Churches were everywhere. All one had to do to get serious about one's faith was find the right church with the programs that fit one's current needs. We expected that if and when the people in our neighborhood wanted to get serious about their faith that they too would just come to church. Underlying it all was this assumption: The Christian life starts with a good church. A good church service first, then the neighborhood.

In the book you have just read, Dan White Jr. turns this on its head. Church does not start with a Sunday service and a list of attractive, felt-needs programs. It starts with the neighborhood. Neighborhood first, then church. Church starts with being present with our neighbors at the intersections of our everyday lives. Dan not only refuses to separate church from the rest of our lives, for Dan church starts there. It starts with our lives taking root in the places we live. The things that once defined church— worship service, programs, etc.—come organically out of our lives rooted in and among our neighbors and our community. For Dan, the future of the church is subterranean.

We must start with the *roots*. In a world where fewer and fewer people go to church, church starts by planting deep roots in community with each other and neighborhoods with real people that are part of our lives. The church is like a slow-growing tree, Dan says. I cannot think of a more important lesson I've learned about church these past twenty-five years than this: that every church must start by submerging deep roots of relationship among a people, a neighborhood, around its tables. This is indeed is where church starts.

Throughout this book Dan has reminded us this new pathway for being the church will be *slow*. We must learn ways to sustain ourselves for the long journey. Every missionary leader of the gospel must come to grips with this. His or her emotional health, ability to stay grounded, his or her entire life will depend upon it. Dan helps us imagine how this might be possible.

Dan tells us *the leader* of this way of church must be chastened of large-church expectations that the modernist churches have become so preoccupied with. Instead, let us be grassroots organizers, slow and steady cultivators, content with some anonymity. Dan exposes the performative contradiction in the ambitions of any Christian teacher, preacher, or blogger who seeks to be the next celebrated leader of his or her generation. This, Dan says, will not result in church. I sense, more and more, that the generations behind me are seeking and searching for what Dan is unpacking in this book and is living in his localized practice. They are already looking for a new imagination for what it means to be the church, faithful to Jesus as Lord, present in North American cities, towns, and villages.

Recently, I was sitting with a group of seminary students in an upstairs apartment in an urban neighborhood talking about ministry. We were tackling the struggles of society, culture, and church. I asked them if they wanted to be pastors when they graduated from seminary. In unison, they all declared a resounding "NO." They were all repulsed by the idea. I was a bit shocked, to say the least. Why then attend seminary? And then I realized what they visualized in their minds when I said the word "pastor." They had in their mind that image of a man or woman wearing their Sunday best, preaching a sermon, and working tirelessly to attract people to their church, serve on their committees, and sign up for their programs. Even if this pastor led a large megachurch with tons of financial resource, these students couldn't see this work as pertinent to the culture of our day. So I changed the question, "What about community organizers of the kingdom? Could you be interested in doing that?" Their response was "Yeahhhhhh." I then reinterpreted the task of a pastor in these terms, as someone who gathered people together in a neighborhood to live into the kingdom of God under the kindness of his reign. This community-organizer leader would gather people to be present to the poor, the hurting, the children, the wandering souls of modernity. Worship would galvanize and fuel imagination for following Christ into the world. By being present to the living Christ in this way, the kingdom would be birthed, and (only) then be organized for mission. With the pastorate reimagined like this, all of us in that room could sense the deep meaning of this kind of expedition.

The struggle for students like those in the apartment that night, as well as many who are passionate about the church, is to reimagine the church's role in the new landscape of America—but they are unsure where and how to start. *Subterranean* is pioneering a path to be trekked for all those Christians who would be community organizers for the kingdom of God. By the mere courageous act of writing it, Dan assures us there are people alongside us ready to begin church as this rooted way of life. What I appreciate about *Subterranean* is its imagination but also its help in providing some immersive tools for the trek. Dan guides us into a reconstruction of the Christian life that is so true that it births kingdom communities of love. Dan not only invites us to rethink church, he invites us into the new world where the incarnation of God in Christ becomes our daily orientation in the world. He helps us see that the future of the church must be subterranean.

And so I say "let the journey begin." Let the grassroots renewal of God's people sprout up across the land. May this book inspire you, as it has inspired me, to the rooted, slow, patient work of cultivating kingdom trees wherever you live.

David E. Fitch
Chair of Evangelical Theology at Northern Seminary
Founding Pastor of Life on the Vine Community

Bibliography

Ackerman, Diane. "Brain on Love." www.opinionator.blogs.nytimes.com/2012/03/24/ the-brain-on.love.

Apfelbaum, E. R. "Memory and Dislocation in the Era of Uprooting." *American Psychologist*, IRM 55 (2000) 108–13.

Aristotle. *Nicomachean Ethics*. Cambridge: Hackett, 2000.

Arpin-Ricci, Jamie. *The Cost of Community: Jesus, St. Francis and Life in the Kingdom*. Downers Grove, IL: InterVarsity, 2011.

Athanasius of Alexandria. *On the Incarnation: Early Church Theology*. New York: Fig, 1960.

"Futuristic & Universal Since 1958." www.atomium.be/History.aspx.

Augustine of Hippo. *The Confessions of St. Augustine*. Colorado Springs: Image Classics, 1960.

Baltimore Lutheran Ministry. "The Revolutionary Table of Jesus." http://www. baltimorelutherancampusministry.org/apps/blog/show/32736062-the-revolutionary-table-of-jesus.

Banks, Robert J. *Paul's Idea of Community*. Grand Rapids: Baker, 1994.

Beatley, T. *Native to Nowhere: Sustaining Home in a Global Age*. Washington, DC: Island, 2004.

Bellah, Robert N., et al. *Habits of the Heart: Individualism and Commitment in American Life*. Berkeley, CA: University of California Press, 1985.

Bessenecker, Scott A. *Overturning Tables: Freeing Missions from the Christian-Industrial Complex*. Downers Grove, IL: InterVarsity, 2014.

Billings, Williams. *Complete Works*. 4 vols. Charlottesville, VA: University of Virginia Press, 1990.

Block, Peter. *Community: The Structure of Belonging*. San Francisco: Berret-Koehler, 2008.

Boesel, Chris, and Catherine Keller, eds. *Apophatic Bodies: Negative Theology, Incarnation, and Relationality*. Bronx, NY: Fordham University Press, 2009.

Botton, Alain de. *Status Anxiety*. London: Hamilton, 2004.

Bonhoeffer, Dietrich. *Life Together: A Classic Exploration of Christian Community*. New York: HarperCollins, 1954.

Boyd, Greg. *God at War: The Bible and Spiritual Conflict*. Downers Grove, IL: InterVarsity, 1997.

Bradley, R. H., and R. E. Corwyn. "Child Trends." *Annual Review of Psychology* 53 (2003) 371–99.

Brewin, Kester. "The Tyranny of Numbers." http://www.kesterbrewin.com/2014/02/13/the-tyranny-of-numbers-obsessive-measurement-demetrification.

———. "The Universe is Not Rigged in Your Favor." https://medium.com/@kesterbrewin/no-rob-bell-the-universe-is-not-rigged-in-your-favor-but-we-can-work-to-rig-it-in-favor-of/.

Burroughs, Nicholas. "Perpetuating Thought." http://www.nicholasburroughs.com/designschooldropout/quouts-perpetuate-thoughs-xvi/.

Cain, Susan. *Quiet: The Power of Introverts in a World that Can't Stop Talking*. New York: Random House, 2012.

Caputo, John. *The Weakness of God: A Theology of the Event*. Bloomington, IN: Indiana University Press, 2006.

Carlyle, Thomas. *Heroes, Hero-Worship and the Heroic in History*. London: Oxford University Press, 1965.

Cassian, John. *Conferences: Classics of Western Spirituality*. Mahwah, NJ: Paulist, 1985.

CBS Atlanta. "Selfie Addiction May Cause Mental Illness." http://atlanta.cbslocal.com/2014/04/09/expert-selfie-addiction-may-cause-mental-illness.

Challies, Tim. "Character is King." www.challies.com/articles/character-is-king.

Chalke, Steve. *Apprentice: Walking the Way of Christ*. Grand Rapids: Zondervan, 2009.

Channing, William Henry. *The Spirit of the Age*. New York: Ulan, 2012.

Cohn, Norman. *The Pursuit of the Millennium*. New York: Oxford University Press, 1970.

Cone, James H. *God of the Oppressed*. Maryknoll, NY: Orbis, 1997.

Costello, J. "Anxiety and Depression in America." *The Journal of Clinical Psychiatry*, 60:7 (1999) 220–67.

Crabb, Larry. *Connecting: Healing for Ourselves and Our Relationships*. Nashville: Word, 1997.

Dana, Daniel. *Conflict Resolution*. Madison, WI: CWL, 2001.

Dawn, Marva J. *Powers, Weakness, and the Tabernacling of God*. Grand Rapids: Eerdmans, 2001.

DeLillo, Don. *White Noise*. New York: Penguin, 1985.

Desilver, Drew. "How Polarized Americans Live Differently." http://www.pewresearch.org/fact-tank/2014/06/13/big-houses-art-museums-and-in-laws-how-the-most-ideologically-polarized-americans-live-different-lives/.

Dossey, Larry. *Space, Time and Medicine*. Berkeley, CA: Shambhala, 1982.

Etymological Dictionary of Modern English. "Radical." www.etymonline.com/index.php?term=radical.

Feldman, R. "Settlement Identity: Psychological Bonds in a Mobile Society." *Global Environmental Change*, 28 (1991) 78–79.

Fenichel, Otto. *The Psychoanalytic Theory of Neurosis*. New York: W. W. Norton, 1945.

Fitch, David E. *The End of Evangelism: Discerning a New Faithfulness for Mission*. Eugene, OR: Cascade, 2001.

———. *The Great Giveaway: Reclaiming the Mission of the Church from Big Business, Parachurch Organizations, Psychotherapy, Consumer Capitalism and Other Modern Maladies*. Grand Rapids: Baker, 2005.

Food and Drug Administration "Vioxx and Drug Safety." www.fda.gov/NewsEvents/Testimony/ucm113235.htm.

Frank, Doug. *A Gentler God: Breaking Free of the Almighty in the Company of the Human Jesus*. Menangle, Australia: Albatross, 2010.

Fretheim, Terence E. *Creation Untamed: The Bible, God, and Natural Disasters.* Grand Rapids: Baker, 2010.

Frost, Michael. *Incarnate: The Body of Christ in an Age of Disengagement.* Downers Grove, IL: InterVarsity, 2014.

Garfield, Charles A. *Peak Performance.* New York: William Morrow, 1986.

Gehring, Roger W. *House Church and Mission: The Importance of Household Structures in Early Christianity.* Peabody, MA: Hendrickson, 2004.

Gonzalez, Justo L. *The Story of Christianity.* New York: Prince, 1984.

Goldman, Jennifer. "Hydraulic Fracturing 101." www.earthworksaction.org/issues/detail/hydraulic_ fracturing_101.

Gombis, Timothy G. "The Apostle Paul: Community Organizer." timgombis.com/2012/09/11/the-apostle-paul-community-organizer.

———. *The Drama of Ephesians: Participating in the Triumph of God.* Downers Grove, IL: InterVarsity, 2010.

———. "Getting Practical About Passive Aggressive Postures." http://timgombis.com/2012/08/28/getting-practical-about-passive-aggressive-postures.

Gorman, Michael J. *Reading Revelation Responsibly: Uncivil Worship and Witness.* Eugene, OR: Cascade, 2010.

Haber, Audrey, and Richard R. Runyon. *Fundamentals of Psychology.* New York: Random House, 1986.

Hammer, Reuven. *The Classic Midrash: Tannaitic Commentaries on the Bible.* Mahwah, NJ: Paulist,1995.

Hauerwas, Stanley. *Approaching the End: Eschatological Reflections on Church, Politics, and Life.* Grand Rapids: Eerdmans, 2013.

———. *Matthew.* Brazos Theological Commentary on the Bible. Grand Rapids: Brazos, 2006.

Hellerman, Joseph H. *When the Church Was a Family: Recapturing Jesus' Vision for Authentic Christian Community.* Nashville: B&H, 2009.

Henson, Jim, and Frank Oz. *The Dark Crystal.* Hollywood: Jim Henson Productions, 1982.

Herbst, Norton and Gabe Lyons. *Where You Live Matters.* Grand Rapids: Zondervan, 2010.

Herper, Matthew. "Merck Withdraws Vioxx." www.forbes.com/2004/09/30/cx_mh_0930merck.html.

Hirsch, Alan. *The Forgotten Ways: Reactivating the Missional Church.* Grand Rapids: Brazos, 2006.

Holland, Joshua. "Pew Research Study: Politically Engaged Liberals and Conservatives Don't Want to Be Neighbors." http://billmoyers.com/2014/06/13/study-politically-engaged-liberals-and-conservatives-dont-want-to-be-neighbors.

Holscaw, Geoff. "The Fall as False Unity: Beginning With Babel." http://www.missioalliance.org/the-fall-as-false-unity-beginning-with-babel.

Honore, Carl. *In Praise of Slowness: Challenging the Cult of Speed.* New York: HarperCollins, 2004.

Janzen, David. *The Intentional Christian Community Handbook.* Brewster, MA: Paraclete, 2013.

Joncas, Jan Michael. *Tasting the Reign of God: The Meal Ministry of Jesus.* St. Paul, MN: Center for Catholic Studies, 2000.

Kempis, Thomas á. *The Imitation of Christ.* Peabody, MA: Hendrickson, 2004.

Kidd, Thomas S. *The Great Awakening: The Roots of Evangelical Christianity in Colonial America.* New Haven, CT: Yale University Press, 2009.

Lewis, C. S. *The Weight of Glory and Other Addresses.* New York: Macmillan, 1949.

Livingston, Ikimulisa. "Stabbed Hero Dies as 20 People Stroll Past Him." www.nypost.com/.../stabbed-hero-dies-as-more-than-20-people-stroll-past-him.

Luhrman, T. M. *When God Talks Back: Understanding the American Evangelical Relationship with God.* New York: Vintage, 2012.

Lupton, Robert D. *Toxic Charity: How Churches and Charities Hurt Those They Help, And How to Reverse It.* San Francisco: HarperOne, 2012.

Manzo, Lynne C., and Patrick Deveine-Wright. "Beyond House and Haven: Toward a Revisioning of Emotional Relationships With Place." *Journal of Environmental Psychology* 43 (2003) 47–52.

———. *Place Attachment.* New York: Routledge, 2014.

Maslow, Abraham. "A Theory of Human Motivation." *Psychological Review* 50 (1943) 370–96.

———. *Toward a Psychology of Being.* Eastford, CT: Martino Fine, 2011.

McKnight, Scot. *The King Jesus Gospel: The Original Good News Revisited.* Grand Rapids: Zondervan, 2011.

———. *A Long Faithfulness: The Case for Christian Perseverance.* Denver: Patheos, 2013.

McKnight, John, and Peter Block. *Abundant Community.* San Francisco: Berret-Koehler, 2010.

McLaren, Brian D. *The Secret Message of Jesus.* Nashville: Thomas Nelson, 2006.

Medical Dictionary. "Asymptomatic Carrier." www.medical dictionary.thefreedictionary.com/asymptomatic+carrier.

Miller, Joel J. "Personal Relationship With Jesus." http://blogs.ancientfaith.com/twocities/personal-relationship-jesus/.

Moss, Michael. *Salt Sugar Fat: How the Food Giants Hooked Us.* New York: Random House, 2013.

Mullainathan, Sendhil. *Scarcity: The Science of Having Less and How it Defines Our Lives.* London: Picador, 2014.

Myers, Ched. *Binding the Strong Man: A Political Reading of Mark's Story of Jesus.* Maryknoll, NY: Orbis, 2011.

Neidzviecki, Hal. *The Peep Diaries: How We're Learning to Love Watching Ourselves and Our Neighbors.* San Francisco: City Light, 2009.

Newbigin, Lesslie. *The Open Secret: An Introduction to the Theology of Mission.* Grand Rapids: Eerdmans, 1995.

Northwestern School of Medicine. "Cognitive Neuroscientists Reveal Creative Brain Processes." www.feinberg.northwestern.edu/news/2004/April/brain_processes.html +&cd=1&hl=en&ct=clnk&gl=us.

Nouwen, Henry. *In the Name of Jesus: Reflections on Christian Leadership.* New York: Crossroad, 1992.

Onondaga Citizens League. "The World at Our Doorstep." Report no. 12, 2012.

Page, David. "Holographic Pastors." http://davepageblog.org/uncategorized/holographic-pastors-2#more-7489.

Pathack, Jay, and Dave Runyan. *The Art of Neighboring.* Grand Rapids: Baker, 2012.

Paul, Greg. *God in the Alley: Being and Seeing Jesus in a Broken World.* Colorado Springs: Waterbrook, 2004.

BIBLIOGRAPHY

Payne, J. D. "Least Churched Cities." North American Mission Board Report (2008) 19–20.

Perriman, Andrew. *The Future of the People of God: Reading Romans Before and After Christendom*. Eugene, OR: Cascade, 2010.

———. "Mission after Christendom: Beyond the Incarnational-Missional Paradigm." www.postost.net/. . ./mission-after-christendom-beyond-incarnational-mission.

Peterson, Eugene. *A Long Obedience in the Same Direction*. Downers Grove, IL: InterVarsity, 2000.

———. *The Pastor: A Memoir*. San Francisco: HarperOne, 2012.

Pew Research Center. "Nones on the Rise." http://www.pewforum.org/2012/10/09/nones-on-the-rise/.

Pollan, Michael. *The Botany of Desire: A Plant's-Eye View of the World*. New York: Random House, 2002.

Pohl, Christine D. *Living Into Community: Cultivating Practices That Sustain Us*. Grand Rapids: Eerdmans, 2012.

Rand, Ayn. *The Virtue of Selfishness*. New York: Signet, 1964.

Reno, R. R. *Genesis*. Brazos Theological Commentary on the Bible. Grand Rapids: Brazos, 2010.

Roberts, Jennifer. "The Power of Patience." harvardmagazine.com/2013/11/the-power-of-patience.

Roxburgh, Alan. *Missional: Joining God in the Neighborhood*. Grand Rapids: Baker, 2011.

Russ, Dan. *Flesh and Blood Jesus: Learning to be Fully Human from the Son of Man*. Grand Rapids: Baker, 2008.

Rutledge, Pamela. "Making Sense of Selfies." https://www.psychologytoday.com/blog/positively-media/201307/making-sense-selfies.

Scandrette, Mark. *Practicing the Way of Jesus: Life Together in the Kingdom of Love*. Downers Grove, IL: InterVarsity, 2001.

Scazzero, Peter. *The Emotionally Healthy Church*. Grand Rapids: Zondervan, 2010.

Schreiter, Robert J. *Constructing Local Theologies*. Maryknoll: Orbis, 1985.

Seamon, David. *A Geography of the Lifeworld*. New York: St. Martins, 1979.

Senge, Peter M. *The Fifth Discipline: The Art and Practice of Learning*. New York: Random House, 1999.

Sharlett, Jeff. *Radiant Truths: Essential Dispatches, Reports, Confessions, and Other Essays on American Belief*. New Haven, CT: Yale University Press, 2014.

Siebert, Wilbur H. *The Underground Railroad from Slavery to Freedom: A Comprehensive History*. Dover, NH: Mineola, 2006.

Skog, Jason. *Yellow Journalism*. Minneapolis: Compass Point, 2007.

Smedes, Lewis. *What God Expects from Ordinary People*. Grand Rapids: Eerdmans, 1989.

Smith, Warren Cole. "Unreal Sales for Mark Driscoll." www.worldmag.com/2014/03/unrealsalesfordriscolls_real_marriage.

Sparks, Paul, Tim Soerens, and Dwight J. Friesen. *The New Parish: How Neighborhood Churches are Transforming Mission, Discipleship and Community*. Downers Grove, IL: InterVarsity, 2014.

Stanley, Andy. *Trust vs. Suspicion*. Audio Sermon. Atlanta: Northpoint Resources, 2012.

Stassen, Glen Harold. *A Thicker Jesus: Incarnational Discipleship in a Secular Age*. Louisville: Westminster John Knox, 2012.

Stump, J. B., and Alan G. Padgett, eds. *The Blackwell Companion to Science and Christianity*. Hoboken, NJ: Wiley-Blackwell, 2012.

Suk, John. *Not Sure: A Pastor's Journey from Faith to Doubt.* Grand Rapids: Eerdmans, 2011.

Surburg, Raymond F. *Introduction to the Intertestamental Period.* Saint Louis: Concordia, 1975.

Susman, Warren. *Culture as History: The Transformation of American Society in the Twentieth Century.* Washington, DC: Smithsonian, 2003.

Taylor-Weiss, Douglas. "What Trees Mean in the Bible." http://m.auburnpub.com/lifestyles/what-trees-mean-in-the-bible-and-in-our-lives/article_cd7ef8bf-b893-5c69-a709-f764c267a076.html?mobile_touch=true.

Tertullian. *Of Patience.* Whitefish, MO: Kessinger, 2010.

Thurian, Max. *The Mystery of the Eucharist.* Grand Rapids: Eerdmans, 1983.

Tickle, Phyllis. *The Great Emergence: How Christianity is Changing and Why.* Grand Rapids: Baker, 2008.

Tolkien, J. R. R. *The Fellowship of the Ring.* New York: Del Rey, 2012.

Trocme, Andre. *Jesus and the Nonviolent Revolution.* Maryknoll, NY: Orbis, 2004.

Tucker, Rod. *Uncovered: The Truth About Honesty and Community.* Grand Rapids: Kregel, 2014.

University Discoveries. "Law of Unintended Consequences." http://university-discoveries.com/the-law-of-unintended-consequences.

Viola, Frank. *Reimagining Church: Pursuing the Dream of Organic Christianity.* Colorado Springs: David C. Cook, 2008.

Virilio, Paul. *Speed & Politics.* Los Angeles: Semiotext, 2006.

Wahm, Athena. "Significant Trees in the Bible and their Symbolisms." http://athena.expertscolumn.com/article/significant-trees-bible-and-their-symbolisms.

Walker, Alice. *In Search of Our Mothers' Gardens: Womanist Prose.* Boston: Mariner, 2003.

Walljasper, Jay. *The Great Neighborhood Book: A Do-it-Yourself Guide to Placemaking.* Gabriola Island, BC: New Society, 2007.

Wardle, Addie Grace. *History of the Sunday School Movement in the Methodist Episcopal Church.* Charleston, SC: Nabu, 2010.

Watts, Nicole. Interview, February 8, 2015.

White, Dan, Jr. "Go Small, Go Missional." http://danwhitejr.blogspot.com/2012/10/go-small-go-missional.html.

———. "The Irritation of Incarnation." http://danwhitejr.blogspot.com/2014/02/the-irritation-of-incarnation.html.

———. "The Numbers Leash." http://danwhitejr.blogspot.com/2014/04/the-numbers-leash.html.

———. "Sabotaging the Hero Complex." http://danwhitejr.blogspot.com/2013/12/sabotaging-hero-complex-in-discipleship.html.

———. "The Source of Community." http://danwhitejr.blogspot.com/2011/02/source-of-community.html.

Whitefield, George. "What Think Ye of Christ?" 1739. www.ccel.org/ccel/whitefield/sermons.xxvi.html.

Wilson-Hartgrove, Jonathan. *The Wisdom of Stability: Rooting Faith in a Mobile Culture.* Brewster, MA: Paraclete, 2010.

Wink, Walter. *Engaging the Powers: Discernment and Resistance in a World of Domination.* Minneapolis: Fortress, 1992.

Wolff, Akiva, and Yonatan Neril. "Trees, Torah, and Caring for the Earth." www.jewcology.com/.../trees-Torah-and-Caring-for-the-Earth.

Woodward, J. R. *Creating a Missional Culture: Equipping the Church for the Sake of the World*. Downers Grove, IL: InterVarsity, 2012.

Wright, David, and Sarah Netter. "Hospital Volunteers Show the Power of Human Touch." http://abcnews.go.com/blogs/headlines/2014/03/cuddling-babies-hospital-volunteers-show-the-power-of-human-touch.

Wright, N. T. *How God Became King: The Forgotten Story of the Gospels*. New York: HarperCollins, 2012.

————. *Mark for Everyone: New Testament for Everyone*. Louisville: Westminster John Knox, 2004.

Yoder, John Howard. *Body Politics: Five Practices of the Christian Community*. Scottdale, PA: Herald, 1992.

————. *Theology of Mission: A Believers Church Perspective*. Downers Grove, IL: InterVarsity, 2014.

Zweig, Paul. *The Heresy of Self-Love*. Princeton, NJ: Princeton University Press, 1968.